The Winners and Losers
in Global Competition

Andreas Sturm
Mathis Wackernagel
Kaspar Müller

The Winners and Losers
in Global Competition

Why Eco-Efficiency Reinforces Competitiveness:
A Study of 44 Nations

Purdue University Press
West Lafayette, Indiana

First U.S. edition published 2004 by Purdue University Press
www.thepress.purdue.edu

First published in German as *Die Gewinner und die Verlierer im globalen Wettbewerb: Warum Öko-Effizienz die Wettbewerbsfähigkeit stärkt: 44 Nationen im Test*, 1999

Printed in the United States of America

ISBN 1-55753-357-1

Cataloging-in-Publication Data available

Contents

List of Figures

List of Tables

List of Abbreviations

FAO	UN Food and Agriculture Organisation
GATT	General Agreement on Tariffs and Trade
GDP	Gross domestic product
ha	Hectare
SGU	Schweizerischen Gesellschaft für Umweltschutz (Swiss Society for Environmental Protection)
UBP	Union Bancaire Privée
USD	U.S. Dollars
WEF	World Economic Forum
WTO	World Trade Organisation

Why the Union Bancaire Privée (UBP) is Sponsoring this Study

Why would one of the largest private banks worldwide sponsor the study presented in this book? Union Bancaire Privée (UBP), headquartered in Geneva, Switzerland, specialises in asset management for private clients and institutions. UBP distinguishes itself among asset managers for sharing with institutional clients the realisation that social and ecological performance can shape the success of long-term investments. As a consequence, its subsidiary, UBP Asset Management, which was founded in 1995 to meet the specific needs of its institutional clients, particularly the Swiss pension funds, has developed an investment strategy for equities and bonds that follows strict criteria of sustainability.

Based on in-depth discussions between clients and a team of experts, UBP Asset Management has translated the abstract idea of sustainability into practical investment criteria and now uses them to manage the funds of its international clients, including the Swiss pension funds. UBP also applied these new criteria of sustainability to redefine benchmarks, performance measurements, and reporting techniques that meet the new requirements of portfolio management.

Today, UBP Asset Management is proud to offer its clients a comprehensive, easily understandable, and clearly structured index for assessing the sustainability of their investments. We are among the first asset managers to apply sustainability screening criteria to government bonds. In this screening, ecological deficits are used as a key indicator for selecting suitable investments. The ecological deficit of a nation represents its ecological draw on nature, by calculating how much its resource use and waste absorption exceed its ecological capacities. The assessments are based on the ecological footprint analysis by Dr. Mathis Wackernagel, one of the authors of this study.

Since September 1998, we have applied this approach in our UBAM-Générations Futures Obligations Internationales fund, which is part of UBP Luxembourg SICAV UBAM. The fund invests worldwide in bonds from states or state organisations that meet the sustainability criteria defined by UBP Asset Management and the fund's advisory council.

Therefore, we are particularly pleased to sponsor this study in which Dr. Andreas Sturm, Dr. Mathis Wackernagel, and financial analyst Kaspar Müller examine the impact of ecological performance on the competitiveness of nations. And we are pleased to find that it substantiates our confidence that the rational use of the earth's assets will eventually strengthen governments' assets, too. However, the study also underscores our concern that the wasteful and careless use of the biosphere's capacity will increasingly harm the perpetrators, whether nations or businesses.

The transition to sustainability is necessary and, in the long term, inevitable. In a world of shrinking resources, those who first recognise the need for sustainability and adopt appropriate strategies will succeed best in future global competition. Directing investment towards sustainability will not only accelerate that transition, but also advance the combined interests of investors, governments, and the public at large. We are pleased to be part of that process.

Contact Address
Union Bancaire Privée (UBP)
96–98, rue du Rhône
CH-1211 Genève 1
Switzerland

UBP Asset Management
8, rue Robert-Estienne
CH-1211 Genève 1
Switzerland

Contact Persons
Mr. Yves Manfrini
E-mail: yma@ubp.ch
Telephone: (0041-22) 819 28 90
Mr. Philippe Lazzarini
E-mail: laz@ubp.ch
Telephone: (0041-22) 819 28 89
Fax: (0041-22) 819 28 95
Website: http://www.ubp.ch

SGU Supports the Study
"The Winners and Losers in Global Competition"

Our dominant culture continues to celebrate blind economic expansion despite its heavy toll on people and nature all over the globe. In fact, our national income accounts (such as the GDP) and our policies ignore that much of today's economic income stems from liquidating our social and natural assets. While living on the planet's capital, rather than on the interest (or sustainable harvest) of its renewable assets, we operate as if we could transgress ecological limits forever. Rather than acknowledging this ecological reality, we actively resist recognising biophysical limits and use wealth to temporarily shield ourselves from the fallout of ecological overshoot. Limits are a taboo. Nevertheless, limits exist. In fact, as the Brundtland Commission of the United Nations pointed out in their 1987 report *Our Common Future,* limits are at the core of the sustainability dilemma. Operating as if these limits did not exist not only diminishes possibilities for the future, but also puts additional pressure on social equity today. How can we develop sustainability initiatives that make sure all can have satisfying lives while we remain within the means of nature? In the opinion of the Schweizerischen Gesellschaft für Umweltschutz (SGU) (the Swiss Society for Environmental Protection), this is the challenge behind sustainability.

We are pleased to see this study addressing this core question of sustainability and showing why nations will also secure their future competitiveness if they improve their ecological performance. These findings are in line with the initiatives our Society has been pursuing over the last decades. The *Schweizerische Gesellschaft für Umweltschutz (SGU)* is an independent environmental organisation with offices in Zurich and Geneva. Since its inception in 1971, it has stimulated dialogue with the business sector, the political arena, and academia on "sustainable development", as it is called today. Also, SGU is represented on the Council for Sustainable Development, an advisory committee of the Swiss government.

The SGU's tangible sustainability initiatives include a network to promote the Local Agenda 21 in Switzerland (which we call "Planet 21") and a campaign to introduce ecological tax reform. In addition, SGU has advocated the creation of a sustainable world by:

- committing to a vision of a sustainable Switzerland that incorporates ecological health, economic vitality, and social well-being.
- developing and setting new priorities – changing our focus from the local to the global, from regulatory environmental protection to economically innovative solutions, from confrontation to co-operation.
- being a source of ideas, a catalyst, and a contact for decisionmakers in politics, business, and society. By providing information and motivation, the SGU helps to shape the future. Its publications and events set new policy directions and provide a social forum for discussions.
- giving competent advice to citizens, authorities, and businesses. It drafts practical strategies for moving towards sustainable development.

In short, the SGU sees no alternative to sustainable development, because it means threefold success: in business, society, and ecology. That's why SGU welcomes this study. It points out succinctly that sustainability is not only inevitable and necessary, but the rational choice for securing the economic vitality of nations and the well-being of their people.

Contact address
Schweizerische Gesellschaft für Umweltschutz (SGU)
Merkustrasse 45 / Postfach
CH-8032 Zurich
Switzerland

Telephone: (0041-1) 251 28 26
Fax: (0041-1) 251 29 41
E-mail: info@sgu.org
Website: http://www.sgu.org

Preface

No one today seriously questions that ecological performance is a key element in the competitiveness and future viability of companies, yet current discussion of the competitiveness of countries largely excludes ecological aspects. The fact that many companies have strengthened their economic position by improving their ecological performance suggests that nations may be able to do the same. Inversely, through poor environmental management, they can jeopardise their future prospects. If this is true, then a country's present ability to generate a high degree of material prosperity within its available ecological capacity is likely to determine its future competitiveness in the global market. Our study supports this view.

The environment both supplies mineral and biological resources and absorbs waste and emissions. However, the biosphere can provide only limited amounts of those ecological services. As expanding human use expends the biosphere's capacity, these ecological services increase in importance. The concept of the ecological footprint, as used in this study, not only enables us to estimate how much nature a country's economy consumes, but also to define the absolute upper limit to consumption – the ecological capacity. The difference between these two values indicates which nations operate above or below their ecological capacity and by how much. We refer to countries that consume less than what their ecological capacity can regenerate as "ecological creditors" because they have ecological remainders – more ecological capacity than they need to produce the resources they consume and absorb the waste they generate. We call countries that consume more nature than their own capacity can provide "ecological debtors."

While ecological debtors (Switzerland, for example) will face a growing economic risk, countries with ecological remainders (like Chile or Sweden) will find this advantage increasingly significant for strengthening their economic performance. It is therefore in the interests of the countries in both categories to reduce their national consumption of nature (or certainly not to increase it). In the short and medium term, debtor countries such as Switzerland can mask their ecological deficit with their financial strength. In the current period of accelerated economic growth, they can afford to pay for their high consumption of resources. Today, to the debtors' advantage, resources continue to decrease in price. This is occurring not because the stock of resources or ecological capacity is increasing, but because more potent technology, trade agreements, and currency convertibility ease access to the remaining stock. For example, GATT free trade agreements, as negotiated under the auspices of the WTO, simplify access to distant resources, while technical improvements in communications and transport make importing resources quicker and easier. Today global resources are depleting more rapidly than ever before due to increasing world trade, the market advantages (historic and current) that industrial nations have over southern countries, and other mechanisms that promote the externalisation of environmental costs and lower the costs of resources. The present situation favours those nations that profit from the externalisation of environmental costs. However, in the long term, countries with ecological debts will become more vulnerable as they become increasingly dependent on countries with ecological reserves. Furthermore, it is unlikely that externalising costs will remain a viable option. International agreements like the climate convention in Kyoto and the many follow-up meetings since will discourage this. Thus, those nations that have high resource consumption compared to their domestic ecological capacity or that use both their own ecological capacity and purchased resources inefficiently may find themselves on the losing side.

Today ecological limits have been reached or exceeded in many areas of the world. At the same time, the realisation that the patterns of consumption and production of industrial nations could never be extended to everybody in the world is becoming more widespread. In environmental and economic policies, the rules of the game are changing – at a local as well as a global level. In the interplay of competition the cards are being reshuffled and dealt anew. The outcome of this process is still open, and the debate on sustainability and the competitiveness of nations has scarcely begun. However, one point is already clear: The winners in today's competition will not necessarily continue to win.

Andreas Sturm
Mathis Wackernagel
Kaspar Müller

Bernhard Vischer and Thomas Pfister have closely read the manuscript and made valuable suggestions. André Tschudin edited the German version of the text. Sue Unwin-Späth translated it into English, and Gary Sue Goodman and Judith Silverstein reworked with the authors the final English text and edited it. We would like to take this opportunity to express our gratitude.

Abstract

This study examines the relationship between the ecological performance and the economic competitiveness of 44 nations. Using the concept of the ecological footprint, the study looks at two aspects of ecological performance. It first assesses the absolute use of biocapacity in each nation. Then it looks at a major factor linking both ecological and economic performance: eco-efficiency, the ratio of economic output (goods and services) to ecological input (such as resources used and wastes absorbed). To measure competitiveness, the study adopts the competitiveness index developed by the World Economic Forum for its annual global competitiveness rankings.

The ecological capacity of a country refers to the ecosystem's limited ability to regenerate the resources the country consumes and to absorb the environmental waste it produces. If this capacity is exceeded, the country becomes dependent on the ecological capacity of other countries; it becomes an "ecological debtor." If, in addition, an ecological debtor also employs its ecological capacity inefficiently, using too much nature to provide too little material wealth, then its future competitiveness becomes compromised in comparison with those nations that manage their resources sparingly and do not overuse their ecological capacity.

Taken together, all the countries studied consume approximately one-third more ecological services than their available ecological capacity can provide, suggesting that the global economy as a whole is poorly positioned for future competition. Still we find that the European countries, Japan, and Canada (this last because of its large ecological remainder) are in distinctly more favourable starting positions for future competitiveness than all the other countries. They are better at using fewer resources to produce commodities, and, in the case of the countries with ecological remainders, they take better care of their existing ecological capacities. Perhaps the most significant finding is that 16 of the 20 eco-efficiency leaders (about 80 percent) are competitive, but only 11 of the 24 eco-efficiency laggards (about 45 percent). This suggests either that eco-efficiency already offers a competitive edge, or that competitiveness and high eco-efficiency are not mutually exclusive.

Introduction and Overview

This study assesses and compares the economic and ecological starting points of various nations, based on relative and absolute ecological performance, thus predicting which countries are likely to win or lose in future competition. To assess economic performance, we adopt the competitiveness index developed by the World Economic Forum for their annual Global Competitiveness Report, which ranks nations according to their economic prospects for the next five to ten years (see http://www.weforum.org/publications). The original contribution of our study is using the ecological footprint concept to assess natural capital and the demands made on it by the economy. We also evaluate the eco-efficiency of nations, which is a major factor in the demand for natural capital. By analysing the relationship between these two assessments, the ecological and the economic, we begin to define, measure, and specify in some detail the factors that determine the sustainable competitiveness of nations.

Defining and Measuring "Sustainable Competitiveness"

The fact that future competition will have to be sustainable is no longer seriously questioned. However, opinions vary widely on exactly what this means. Before we judge the ecological positioning of a country, let us first clarify the concept of sustainability. We believe that sustainability requires living within the means of nature. This is the ecological imperative for sustainability. In other words, the world population as a whole must not use more resources or cause more environmental damage than the biosphere can tolerate. To do otherwise means depleting the world's natural capital by exceeding its regenerative capacity. In economic terms, the basic goal is to maintain natural capital, the natural "assets" with which humanity is endowed. By living off the "interest," we could hand down to the next generation a stock of natural assets equivalent to those that the present generation received from its predecessors.

As simple as this basic concept appears, its implementation poses a number of challenges. First, we need to know the availability and use of natural assets. Once the problem of measuring and taking inventory has been solved, strategies must be developed to keep human use of nature within the bounds of the biosphere's regenerative capacity. In other words, humanity must strive to maintain the quality, quantity, and regenerative ability of natural capital stock and to increase it wherever possible. This is no easy task. Most likely, it will require that all countries endorse global measures for sustainability. Still, as we show in this study, many steps necessary for global sustainability may actually be in the countries' self-interest. If they want to remain competitive, they may find it advantageous to adopt such sustainability measures even before a global agreement emerges.

The Ecological Footprint and Ecological Capacity
The ecological footprint concept offers a promising starting point for the assessment of available natural capital and the demands made on it by an economy's production or consumption (Wackernagel and Rees 1996). Using Wackernagel's method of calculating the ecological footprint, it is possible to quantify the stock of natural assets or ecological capacity. The footprint calculation also allows us to quantify both global and national demands on nature (more detail on this begins on page 27).

The extent to which a nation consumes products and services determines its demand on ecological capacity. Since this consumption requires resources and produces waste, it directly depends on nature's services. This use of nature corresponds to the "ecological footprint."

Ecological Debtors and Creditors
By comparing nations' ecological footprints with their ecological capacity, we can distinguish between countries that consume more nature than they have and those that use less nature than they have. In this way, we can divide the national economies of the world into two categories. By analogy with terms commonly used

in economics, we refer to one category as "ecological debtors" and the other as "ecological creditors." This analysis reveals which countries live at the cost of others and which countries make their remainder of natural capital available for others (the selling countries, or, in economic terms, the creditors). The sum of the countries' footprints and capacities shows that they operate with ecological deficit, and evidence suggests that all the world's economies taken together are also in such a debtor position (Wackernagel et al. 1999a).

Since the earth's inhabitants cannot import ecological capacity from other planets, today's world economies operate by liquidating rather than maintaining their most essential asset: natural capital (this is explained further below, beginning on page 31).

Overshoot: The Forgotten Core Concept of Sustainability

Ecological limits are not like a rigid wall that brings a speeding car to a grinding halt. Rather, ecological limits can be transgressed easily. More timber can be harvested than regrows, more fish can be caught than are spawned, more CO_2 can be emitted than nature can reabsorb, and more fresh water can be pumped out of the ground than is being replenished. And initially, such transgressions go unnoticed.

Emerging academic disciplines are now starting to focus on this challenge. For example, ecological economics stands out for recognising the need to keep the scale of the economy small enough to fit within the biosphere. It emphasises that we need to live on the interest of the earth's natural capital rather then dipping into the capital. If we take more than the interest, humanity moves into overshoot: exceeding nature's capacity and thereby diminishing its ability to regenerate. Such ecological overshoot is possible – indeed happening – and highly undesirable.

The importance of avoiding overshoot has become a central theme of the ecological economics discipline, but is still ignored not only in general conversations but also in many public policy discussions of sustainability. In fact, our ability to transgress ecological limits without perceptible consequences may create the most influential misconceptions of the sustainability debate. For example, in a recent interview on reaching a world population of 6 billion, Nafis Sadik, executive director of the UN Population Fund, stated that "many environmentalists think [that the carrying capacity of the earth] is four billion, maximum. But now we have six billion people."[1]

However, ecological economists know that this apparent contradiction is a fallacy. The reality is that ecological limits can be exceeded for some time because nature reacts with some inertia. More precisely, natural capital can be harvested faster than it regenerates, thereby depleting the capital stock. Ecologists have observed such "overshoot dynamics" with many species – and human civilisations. In fact, declaring that current levels of consumption can be maintained since we are already consuming at this rate reminds us of the warped logic of a joke. It sounds like the dare devil jumping from the 40th floor, declaring while passing the 10th floor that he is perfectly safe, since so far nobody got hurt.

Indeed, it is possible that human consumption is waxing, as pointed out by economist Julian Simon, while ecological capacity is waning, as pointed out by environmentalist Norman Myers.[2] Overshoot explains why these two story lines are not in contradiction, but two sides of the same coin. There may be dispute over what the consequences of prolonged overshoot may be. Some fear that human overshoot can follow the dynamics of fisheries, where unsustainable harvests can trigger rapid and systemic collapse of ecosystems and leave the resource stock irreversibly damaged. Others hope that the contraction of ecosystem services will be slower and more forgiving. However, no ecological economists would argue that overshoot is inconsequential.

Worse, there are no corrective forces working against overshoot. In the modern industrial world, "sustainable limits" can easily be exceeded, because potential constraints imposed by increasingly scarce resources and increased efforts to extract them are masked by technological advances, cheap energy sources, and easier access to distant resources. Feedback is particularly weak on the waste side: For example, CO_2 leaves tail pipes with ease, independent of the CO_2 concentration in the atmosphere.

This is why systematic resource accounting is so crucial to sustainability. As long as our governments and business leaders do not know how much nature we use or how resource use compares to the existing stocks, overshoot may go undetected – increasing the ecological debt of society.

The "Big Feet" and the "Little Feet"

Computing the per capita footprints of the nations in our study reveals significant differences among countries. Some countries – we call them the "big feet" – use an above-average share of nature per capita. In contrast are those countries with a below-average utilisation of nature, the "little feet." Which category a nation falls into depends not only on its level of consumption but also on the methods and technology used in its production, its transportation of products, and disposal infrastructures (for further detail, see page 37 onwards).

The "Heavyweights" and "Lightweights"

Population is a significant factor in the size of a country's footprint. We use the terms "heavy weights" and "lightweights" to describe nations whose footprints are relatively large or small due to population or high per capita consumption. If the population figures of a country are included in this examination, it becomes apparent that four nations alone – the U.S.A., India, China, and Russia – are responsible for over half of the collective footprint of the countries in this study (more on page 39 onwards).

The Sustainability of the Gross Domestic Product

Despite their similarly large population sizes, these four countries show significant differences, particularly in terms of material wealth per capita. This wealth disparity impacts the socio-economic dimension of sustainability. Most obviously in this respect, material wealth cannot be limited to a mere few: Those people at the lower end of the material wealth scale legitimately expect to gain increased access to material wealth. However, this poses a dilemma. The world as a whole already operates beyond its ecological capacity. Therefore, the only way out is to achieve economic performance with as little use of ecological services as possible – that is, with the smallest possible ecological footprint. If we ask ourselves how much gross domestic product we can produce within the bounds of our own ecological capacity, we see that the majority of industrialised countries could achieve only a fraction of their present economic performance using their own ecological capacity. For the

missing part, such nations depend on a net import of foreign ecological capacity. For these countries to operate more sustainably,
they can embark on three fundamental courses of action: reduce
gross domestic product (which depends on reducing per capita
consumption and population numbers over time – both challen-
ging but probably inevitable long-term strategies); increase eco-efficiency ("produce the same with less," that is, use a smaller ecological footprint for the production of material wealth); or import
capacity from countries with ecological remainders (more on page
41 onwards).

The Ecological "Bulls" and "Bears"

So far we have dealt with the starting positions in ecological and
material terms. We now bring another factor into play: the competitiveness of nations. We base our assessment on a widely recognised
unit of measure – the competitive index of the World Economic
Forum (WEF 1997) – and relate this variable to the ecological
footprint of a country, looking at both ecological capacity and ecological efficiency.

By analogy with the terms used in the financial markets for rising
prices or markets in which traders expect prices to rise, we call the
competitive countries "bulls" and the noncompetitive countries
"bears." To describe the ecological status, we refer to countries that
remain within their ecological capacity (ecological creditors) as
"green" and to those that exceed it (ecological debtors) as "red."
Thus, we can divide the nations in our study into four categories:

- *Green bulls:* Nations attaining a high degree of competitiveness while still
  operating within their ecological capacity; these are ecological creditors who
  are also economically successful.
- *Red bulls:* Nations attaining an equally high degree of competitiveness, but
  which operate beyond their ecological limits; these are economic successes
  but ecological debtors.
- *Green bears:* Nations with a low competitiveness ranking but an ecological
  surplus; these are struggling economically but are ecological creditors.

> • *Red bears:* Nations with both a low competitiveness ranking and ecological
>   debt; these are both struggling economically and accumulating ecological
>   debt.
>
> (See page 46 for more explanation.)

Green bears are extremely rare animals. Without exception, the countries in our study that are endowed with large ecological capacity, yet who fail to be economically competitive, are suffering or recovering from violent internal conflicts. They include Colombia and Brazil. On the opposite extreme, there are quite a few red bulls such as Holland, Switzerland, Singapore, and Japan.

At first glance, the number of red bulls might seem to contradict our thesis that ecological risk translates into economic risk. But this is not the case, and it is easy to explain why. All these countries have had a historic advantage. They could accumulate financial capital at a time when ecological capacity was not as scarce, and their technological advantages helped them to expand their economies. Now they can afford to buy access to the ever-scarcer resources in financially poorer countries. The red bears will experience the greatest difficulty reaching a strong and sustainable economy. Sustainability in these countries requires structural economic changes whose achievement is rendered difficult by the very competitive disadvantage they seek to overcome (more detail begins on page 46).

The "Eco-Efficiency Leaders" and the "Eco-Efficiency Laggards"
One of the essential factors in determining competitiveness is productivity or, in more general terms, the efficiency of a national economy. Since conventional productivity factors (such as productivity of labour) are already included in the competitive index of the World Economic Forum, we look somewhat further and ask what size footprint is needed to generate one unit of the gross domestic product. We will describe this ratio as eco-efficiency. Above-average performers in this respect are mainly found among the European countries. We call them "eco-efficiency leaders." On the other

end of the spectrum are the stragglers, whom we describe as "eco-efficiency laggards." The latter use a disproportionately large amount of nature to generate one unit of their gross domestic product. Among this group are countries of the former Eastern Bloc, for instance, but also industrialised countries such as the U.S.A. (more detail on this begins on page 51).

Eco-Efficiency and Ecological Capacity: Green and Red Leaders and Laggards

Ecological inefficiency is worrisome mainly for countries that already operate outside their ecological capacity. These "red eco-efficiency laggards" rely either on importing ecological capacity, with all the financial drawbacks this entails, or on subjecting their economy to a drastic eco-efficiency recovery program (further information begins on page 55).

Eco-Efficiency and Competitiveness: Efficient and Inefficient Bulls and Bears

Here the question arises, are the more eco-efficient countries also more competitive? To shed light on this issue, we looked at the relationship between the eco-efficiency and the competitiveness of nations, grouping them into four categories:

- Competitive countries with above-average eco-efficiency (efficient bulls);
- Competitive countries with below-average eco-efficiency (inefficient bulls);
- Noncompetitive countries with above-average eco-efficiency (efficient bears);
- Noncompetitive countries with below-average eco-efficiency (inefficient bears).

What we see is that virtually all the countries with high eco-efficiency also have a high degree of competitiveness. We call this group the "efficient bulls." Conversely, most of the "eco-efficiency laggards" have a low degree of competitiveness. Hence we call them "inefficient bears." Some countries with a large ecological ca-

pacity are the exception, because they can "afford" their inefficiency by drawing on their abundant ecological capacity without
immediately losing their competitiveness. These "inefficient bulls"
are very rare, however. The situation looks less rosy for the noncompetitive and inefficient countries – the "inefficient bears" –
where the enhanced competitiveness must go hand in hand with an
eco-efficiency revolution. This is true mainly for countries that
have no ecological capacity reserves (more beginning on page 58).

Winners and Losers of the Competition

It is mainly the European countries, Japan, and Canada (the last
because of its vast ecological reserves) who will be the winners of
the future competition. To enhance their competitiveness, all other
countries must deal more efficiently with nature and take better
care of their available ecological capacities (more on this and the
list of winners and losers beginning on page 63).

Environmental Strategies at the Beginning of the Millennium

Competitive policy dictates that countries must, to a much greater
extent than they do now, use modern environmental policy strategies in addition to new ones: Nations must improve the way they
handle their own ecological capacity and their eco-efficiency. We
will ultimately succeed in implementing sustainability only if we
begin in our own backyard, at the same time intensifying international co-operation and focusing the efforts of all social groupings,
including government and businesses. Everything else is patch-
work, detrimental to each nation's own competitiveness, and, hence,
to each nation's own prosperity (see page 67 for further detail).

How Sustainably do Nations Operate?

In a global free-market economy, a nation's competitiveness plays a decisive role in its ability to maintain or increase its material prosperity. So far, the political focus has been on allowing national and international business as much free rein as possible and on supporting this development with investments in infrastructure and education. Dealing efficiently with the environment has not so far been considered a specific goal in economic policy and strategy. That is why the use of nature as a production and consumption factor is extremely inefficient. Aggravated by unmitigated economic growth, this inefficiency necessarily leads to an overuse of the world's limited capacity.

The further we go beyond this capacity limit, the more the efficient handling of resources becomes a crucial competitive factor. The reasons for this are varied: increasing social demand for a healthy environment, more strict implementation of international environmental agreements, more use of pricing instruments for environmental policy, increasing reluctance of countries to overuse their own environments, and decreasing tolerance of countries for other nations' exploiting their ecological assets.

Eco-Efficiency

Eco-efficiency, a concept developed in the eighties, was first used by the chemical industry (Schaltegger and Sturm 1989, 1990). During the nineties, the World Business Council for Sustainable Deve-lopment promoted the concept so successfully that now a large number of companies worldwide support the concept (WBCSD 1996; Schmidheiny 1992).
Eco-efficiency is defined as the ratio of economic performance (real net output) to the input of ecological services, such as resources provided, environmental pollution generated, and waste absorbed. Eco-efficiency links economic efficiency and environmental performance. While maximising eco-efficiency is a common business strategy and central tenet of corporate philosophy and corporate culture, converting this concept into measurable quantities has been problematic. At the corporate level, this measurement approach has largely been

successful [UNCTAD/Ellipson 1998]. At the country level, this publication is a first attempt to link the concept of the ecological footprint (which is highly suitable for this issue) with economic variables (for more on the ecological footprint, refer to page 27).

If we could attain the existing level of material prosperity with fewer natural resources, and continue to do so over the long term, the problem of overuse could be solved. In the future, this eco-efficiency strategy (see the box above) must play a decisive role in the economic development of nations, if they wish to safeguard their material wealth and freedom of action. Eco-efficiency is even more important when we consider that the inefficient use of nature will lead to scarcity and hence create higher costs in the twenty-first century. In certain countries and with respect to certain resources (for example, water or landfill space), eco-efficient strategies are already in practice and showing financial benefits. If this trend continues – and there are good reasons to assume that it will – the more eco-efficient nations will have a head start in the international race.

In the future, those countries will be on the losing side that:
• live beyond their means; that is, use more ecological services than their own territory provides in a sustainable manner (ecological debtors).
• use ecological services in a wasteful way; that is, use a disproportionately large amount of these services per unit of gross domestic product.
• have consumption patterns that depend on an excessive amount of ecological services.

The more such weak points a country has, the sooner it will suffer in competition with other nations.

To analyse this relationship, we sought to determine the eco-efficiency of nations. A total of 44 countries, generating almost three-quarters of the worldwide gross domestic product, were analysed in terms of the following questions:

- Does the country operate below or above its ecological capacities? In other words, is the country an ecological debtor or an ecological creditor?
- How much ecological capacity does the country use to reach a certain level of material wealth? In other words, does the country have a high or a low eco-efficiency?

We placed these questions in a wider economic and developmental context by considering issues such as the competitive position, population, and income level of each country. The selection of the countries is based on practical considerations such as data availability or quality. Due to the lack of data, especially on competitiveness, African and Arab countries could not be included.

Measuring Human Use of Nature with the Ecological Footprint

Nature supplies us with all requirements for life. Thanks to its production and regeneration of resources and ecological services, we have energy for heating and transportation; timber for buildings, furniture, and paper; and food and clean water for sustenance. Plants use photosynthesis to convert sunlight, carbon dioxide, minerals, and water into biochemical energy. This plant biomass forms the basis for all food chains – on which all animals, including humans, depend. As resources are consumed, nature also absorbs the waste that is generated and secures vital functions such as climatic stability, water and nutrient cycles, and genetic continuity. We humans are embedded in nature and fully dependent on it.

As we use nature's products and services, we also put it under stress. This is only natural. It is physically inevitable and not really anything to worry about, as long as our use of nature does not exceed the biosphere's capacity to regenerate. But this is exactly what we are doing: Our use of nature now exceeds its regenerative capability.

The concept of the ecological footprint was developed to estimate people's impact on nature (Wackernagel and Rees 1996). It does this by measuring how much bioproductive area is required to support today's consumption in the long term. Ecological footprint calculations are based on two fundamental insights: First, we can keep fairly accurate accounts of most of the resources we use and of the waste we generate; and second, most of these resource and waste flows can be combined and quantified as the biologically productive area needed to provide them.

This means that the ecological footprint of individuals, nations, or even the world becomes measurable. Thus the footprint is the area of biologically productive land and sea surface required to provide resources and to absorb the waste produced when using them – given the prevailing technology today. Many rich countries import a significant part of their resources from all over the world. They also export waste that impacts faraway places (often informally through pollutants in the air or waterways). The footprint of nations adds up all these areas wherever they are on the globe, taking into account a country's imports (which are added to its footprint) and exports (which are subtracted).

Our calculations, which are based on public domain statistics of the United Nations (Wackernagel et al. 1999a), show that in 1993, the average Canadian needed just short of 7 hectares of bio-productive land and about 1 hectare of ocean surface to keep up his or her personal level of consumption. The average Canadian therefore needed 7.7 hectares or 77,000 square metres (770 by 100 metres) of bio-productive land – that is, more than 18 football fields. The average American in 1993 lived in even greater material splendour: Her footprint was 30 percent larger. The average Italian occupied with his consumption half the ecological area a Canadian requires. Both the Swiss and the Germans lived, on average, on about 5 hectares.

This area is calculated from the net consumption of some 45 different major resources, adjusted for trade, using figures derived from the trade and production statistics supplied by the United Nations. The calculation is completed by an analysis of the nation's energy consumption. In order to compute the true consumption of the nation, the calculation includes an estimate of the energy embodied in the country's net imports. Taking into account the types of energy being used, this consumed energy is then converted into the corresponding footprint areas. An example of this computation for Italy is available on the Internet.[3] Since we assumed optimistic biological yields for the calculations, and since we were unable to include some uses of nature into our calculations, these values are rather conservative: The bio-productive areas that are really needed to maintain today's usage of nature's benefits are most probably larger.

Finding Our Limits

If we divide the whole surface of the earth's bio-productive land and sea by the number of people living today, we arrive (for 1998) at a statistical average of 2.2 hectares of bio-productive area per person of the world's population (i.e., 22,000 square metres). Of these 2.2 hectares, 1.7 hectares are natural or manipulated land-based ecosystems (forests, meadows, and arable land) and 0.5 hectares are productive ocean surface (mainly coastal areas and continental shelves). These calculations of eco-capacity are based on data by the UN Food and Agriculture Organisation (FAO). In order to make the results directly comparable, we have expressed the bio-capacities and the ecological footprints of all countries in the same measuring unit: bio-productive area with world average yield.

Existing Applications of the Footprint Concept

By providing ways to assess potential trade-offs, the ecological footprint becomes a yardstick for measuring the ecological bottom line of sustainability – a precondition for satisfying lives. The tool has provided the stimulus and foun-

dation for many courses and thesis projects at universities all over the world.[4]
More important, it has informed discussions and debates from the global level
to the local scale by national governments, UN meetings, research institutes, and
municipal green plan initiatives[5] to name a few.[6] In addition:

- global and national studies have compared countries' overall consumption to
  their eco-capacities or analysed the ecological capacity embodied in trade.[7]
- municipal footprints have been computed and sustainability strategies eva-
  luated with the footprint tool.[8]
- individual impacts at the household scale have been assessed with a variety
  of calculators, including software programs explicitly designed for adoption
  in school curricula.[9]
- product footprints or the ecological demands of the cumulative effects of specific consumer items have also been compared using the footprint method.[10]

This method of ecological accounting helps planners in organisations, corpora-
tions, and public administrations to put the use of nature by a population in relation to the existing natural capacities. In other words, the footprint shows the
ecological load of the human population in relation to the eco-capacity of the
biosphere. This allows us to monitor people's ecological performance, to identify the challenges for reducing our ecological footprints, and to document the
gains on the way to sustainability. The ecological footprint is thus a tool for developing, testing, and implementing strategies for a sustainable future.

Now there is another slight complication: For reasons of ecological
stability alone, we humans should not use the entire 2.2 hectares
for ourselves. After all, we share this planet with over 10 million
other species of animals and plants. Most of these species we exclude
from the ecosystems we occupy because we consider them to be
competitors; in agriculture, for instance, we speak of "weeds" and
"pests," meaning those species we cannot exploit commercially or
economically. We also exclude other species when we seal some of
the most fertile cropland under concrete and tarmac. This is why
we should ask ourselves how much of the earth's bio-productive
area we should leave fallow and uncultivated for the other 10 million species.

Only very few of the many people we asked believe that we should
leave less than a third of the worldwide bio-productive area to

other species (i.e., two-thirds for us humans, one-third for the rest). In contrast, with the practices we employ today, we push many of these species to the edge of survival or even to extinction. In order to be as generous as possible to humans and to make sure that we do not overstate the ecological scarcity of this planet, our footprint calculations follow the politically bold, but ecologically inadequate[11] proposal made by the Brundtland Commission in its 1987 report, *Our Common Future.* The Commission proposed to the world community that we should protect 12 percent of the planet's bio-productive area for the other 10 million species. Using this far too conservative figure, the area available for each of the earth's human inhabitants would drop to 2 hectares. With the expected growth figures, the world population will reach 10 billion before the year 2050. This would mean that every inhabitant of the earth would, on average, have as little as 1.2 hectares available, including the productive ocean surface.

Ecological Debtors and Creditors

The average Italian alone uses more than double what the world population is entitled to per person – and three times more than Italy's ecosystems can sustainably offer. Italy is therefore an "ecological debtor," in our definition, a country that requires more resources to cover its consumption than it actually has under its own long-term capacity. Sweden is ecologically better off; it is among the small group of lucky nations whose eco-capacity today exceeds their footprints. We call these countries "ecological creditors" (Figure 1)[12].

The world as a whole belongs to the category of ecological debtors, because humanity's footprint exceeds the world's eco-capacity by one-third, if we exclude from possible use the meagre 12 percent for preserving the diversity of species. In other words, people consume more than nature can provide in the long run. Humanity is therefore depleting the world's natural capital. And this is where the great challenge of sustainability lies: "How can we assure quality of life for all within less than 2 hectares per person?" This is probably the most important question faced in science, business, and politics today. The quantitative goal of 2-hectare footprints per person on average (at current population levels) becomes a tangible and necessary goal for sustainability, and a specific benchmark to which current performance can be compared.

The category of ecological debtors includes countries such as Germany, Japan, and the U.S.A., but also lower income countries like India or Russia. These nations operate with an ecological deficit and therefore live by depleting their own natural capital assets or by exploiting the eco-capacity of other countries. The objection that these nations do, after all, pay for their additional need in eco-capacity is untenable because environmental costs (or externalities, as they are called by economists) are rarely, if at all, considered in prices. In the long term (particularly as more of the externalities will be internalised in prices), ecological debtors are therefore more likely to also become economic debtors. It is only the far-reaching externalisation of environmental costs that allows these countries to continue accumulating ecological debts without ever having to settle these accounts.

Figure 1: Ecological Creditors and Debtors (by country)

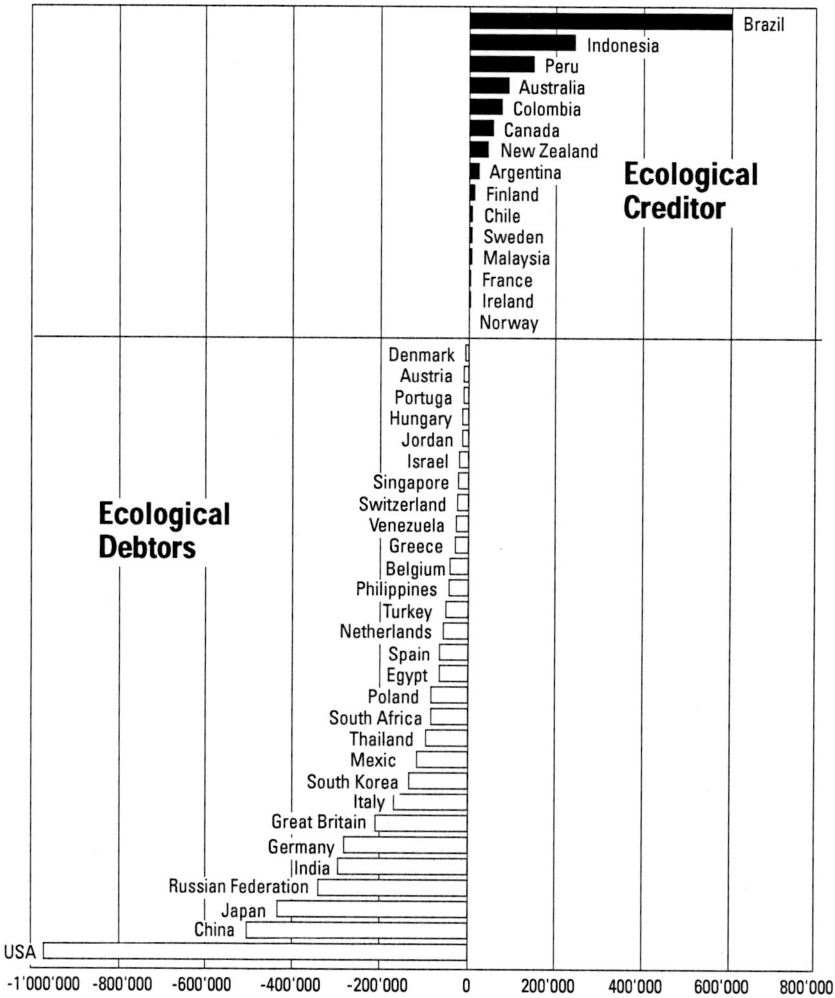

Brazil
Indonesia
Peru
Australia
Colombia
Canada
New Zealand
Argentina
Finland
Chile
Sweden
Malaysia
France
Ireland
Norway

Ecological Creditor

Denmark
Austria
Portuga
Hungary
Jordan
Israel
Singapore
Switzerland
Venezuela
Greece
Belgium
Philippines
Turkey
Netherlands
Spain
Egypt
Poland
South Africa
Thailand
Mexic
South Korea
Italy
Great Britain
Germany
India
Russian Federation
Japan
China
USA

Ecological Debtors

-1'000'000 -800'000 -600'000 -400'000 -200'000 0 200'000 400'000 600'000 800'000

Remainder of Ecological Capacity (in 1000 ha per

The ecological capacity of Brazil exceeds its use of nature (as measured by the ecological footprint) by approximately 600 million hectares. This makes Brazil the ecological creditor with the largest ecological remainder among the nations analysed. In contrast, the United States ranks as the country with the largest ecological deficit since its bioproductive space is close to 1 billion hectares smaller than its footprint (1993 data).

But who, then, is paying the debt? Globally, the bill is picked up to-day partly by those nations that live below their maximum ecological capacity. Future generations will have to foot the rest of the bill.

The category of ecological creditors includes countries such as Brazil, Colombia, Peru, Chile, Argentina, and Canada on the American continent; Indonesia and Malaysia in Asia; Finland, Sweden, Ireland, and Norway in Europe; and Australia and New Zealand. These countries are clearly in the minority, with Brazil being by far the largest ecological donor country in spite of the (probably justified) criticism of its forest use. The following question must be asked: What right do the ecological debtor countries have to demand that donor countries reduce their footprints, particularly since there is no equivalent commitment on the part of the debtors?

The ecological creditors subsidise the debtors voluntarily only to a limited degree. The ever-increasing deregulation of world trade also increases global competitive pressure, which is today working against efforts to internalise externalities. Since there are no world-wide ecological rules of the game, some countries are forced to squander their resources because they would otherwise lose in prosperity compared with their rivals and, as a rule, would also lose jobs. This, in turn, pressures politicians to avoid economic policies that are more in line with sustainability. As long as globalisation continues to favour externalisation of ecological costs, progress towards combining economic competitiveness with ecological sustainability will be slow and difficult. However, if our analysis is correct, taking ecological performance seriously has a positive effect on a nation's competitiveness even today.

If one calculates the per capita ecological capacity of a country, there is a slight shift in the picture of ecological debtors and creditors (Figure 2). Densely populated countries such as Singapore fare somewhat worse, while thinly populated countries such as New Zealand fare somewhat better. What is remarkable is that the U.S.A. is at the bottom of the list from both points of view. But the ecological debts per person are only marginally lower in models of eco-efficiency in countries such as Germany and Switzerland because of the low ecological capacity of these countries.

But all the reserves of ecologically rich nations added together are still not enough to compensate for the eco-deficit run up by other nations. Indeed, taken together the nations of the world are running up debts at the expense of future generations – an insight which in itself is not all that new but which this analysis confirms in quantitative terms.

Figure 2: Ecological Creditors and Debtors (per capita)

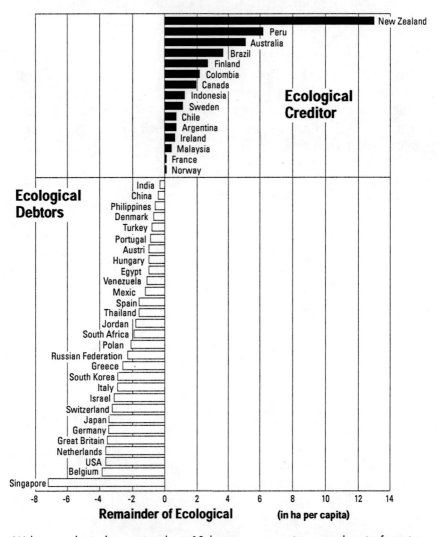

With an ecological capacity about 13 hectares per capita more than its footprint, New Zealand is endowed with the largest ecological remainder. Not surprisingly, this ranking reflects to some extent the density of the countries' inhabitants. Singapore, with hardly any bioproductivity per capita, needs to import its entire footprint and has the largest per capita ecological deficit among the countries analysed. Similarly, the inhabitants of densely populated, highly industrial countries such as Germany, Switzerland, and Japan also have footprints larger than their national capacities (1993 data).

"Big Feet" and "Little Feet"

Whether a country is an ecological debtor or a creditor is determined by two factors: its ecological capacity and its ecological footprint. The larger and more productive the area of a country, the larger its ecological capacity. This is more or less predetermined by natural conditions and circumstances. But the average ecological footprint is determined by the level of consumption and the methods of production. The ecological capacity per person is dictated by the surface area of a country, the bio-productivity of that surface, and the number of inhabitants.

In the average country included in the study, every person needed 2.65 hectares to satisfy its consumer needs. But, as we established above, the global per capita capacity available is only 2 hectares. Looking at per capita footprint, the footprint of an individual in a given country under the conditions prevailing there, our analysis distinguishes two groups of countries:

- ecological "big feet" or countries whose inhabitants leave relatively large footprints.
- ecological "little feet" or countries that leave relatively small footprints.

Measured against the average of all the countries analysed, big feet have a disproportionately large footprint per person of the population, whereas little feet have a disproportionately small footprint (Figure 3).

Figure 3: Ecological «Little Feet» and «Big Feet»

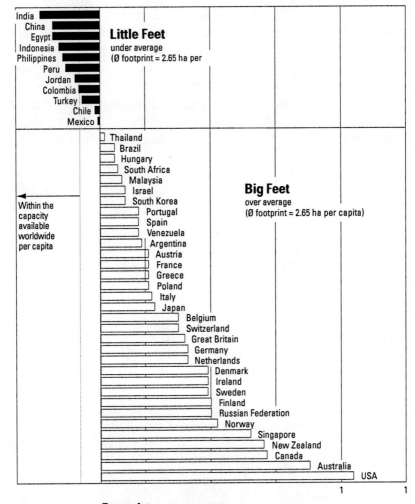

Footprint (in ha per capita)

In the global average, a person requires about 2.65 hectares of bioproductive area. However, taking the capacity into consideration, to avoid overshoot the average person at current population levels should not occupy a footprint larger than 2 hectares. This analysis shows that low-income countries are far more likely to have tiny footprints while highly industrialised countries with low population density, such as Australia, Canada, New Zealand, and the United States, have larger footprints (1993 data).

People in less prosperous countries such as China or India live on relatively small ecological footing. A brief comparison: The footprint of an average inhabitant of the U.S.A. is about 13 times larger than that of a person in India. If the difference in life expectancy is also taken into account, we find that an inhabitant of the United States uses as much as 18 times more of the earth's productive area than an Indian does. This way of looking at things casts a new light on the problem of overpopulation: Every baby born in the U.S.A. will use as much "earth" in its lifetime as 18 children born in India. Seen from this angle, it is not primarily India that is overpopulated – but the U.S.A.

"Heavyweights" and "Lightweights"

If we now focus our attention on the size of national populations, we can tell which countries are placing the greatest strain on the environment (Figure 4 and Figure 5).

Figure 4: Ecological «Lightweights» and «Heavyweights»

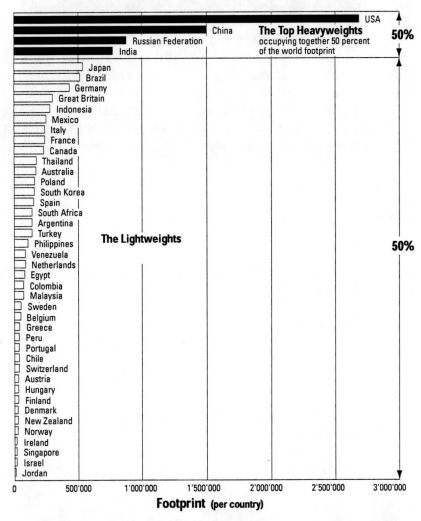

Footprint (per country)

Figures 4 and 5: Four countries — the United States, China, the Russian Federation, and India — occupy together over 50 percent of the total footprint. This does not seem too dramatic at first glance since these countries also represent 61 percent of the total population. Once we consider the distribution of population and footprints, however, the picture gets more accentuated. The United States, with 6 percent of the total population, is responsible for 25 percent of the total footprint. For the Russian Federation, with 3 percent of the world population and 8 percent of the total footprint, the contrast is less stark. The opposite, however is happening with China and India. Their combined population represents 52 percent of the world's total, while their share of the total footprint is only 20 percent.

Figure 5: Footprint and Population in a Global Perspective

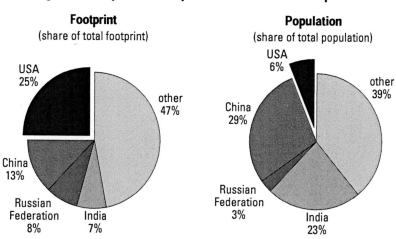

Footprint
(share of total footprint)

Population
(share of total population)

Only four countries – we call them "heavyweights" – are responsible for more than 50 percent of the entire footprint. This is particularly staggering in the case of the U.S.A., because that country accounts for only 6 percent of the population, but causes 25 percent of the total footprint (a similar, but less dramatic situation prevails in Russia with 3 percent of the population and 8 percent of the footprint).

The reverse situation is equally worrisome. The two most populous countries analysed – India and China – account for just about 50 percent of the population and 20 percent of the total footprint. Taking into account the low level of material consumption and income in both these countries and their economic growth prospects, the likely per capita increase in the footprint in both countries would have dramatic ecological effects.

Sustainable Gross Domestic Product

If we now look at the issue of ecological debtors and creditors from an economic perspective, we may ask the following question:

Assuming today's consumption and production conditions, how high should the gross domestic product (GDP) of a country be to correspond to a footprint that is commensurate with the country's ecological capacity? In other words, what percentage of the gross domestic product can be produced and consumed if the country moves within its ecological limits, that is, is neither debtor nor creditor (Figure 6)?[13] We describe this percentage as the GDP sustainability rate.

Figure 6: Domestic Ecological Capacity to Sustain GDP

(maximum GDP that the domestic ecological capacity could sustain — or the
percentage of current economic activities the domestic ecosystems could fuel)

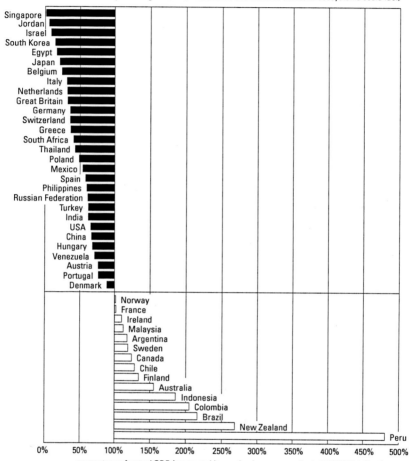

percentage of actual GDP (measured in purchasing-power-adjusted 1993 US dollars)

If countries were allowed to produce only as much GDP as their domestic ecological capacity allows, the majority could not maintain their current level of economic activities. This measure represents to what extent a country's footprint can be accommodated by its domestic ecological capacity. By «domestic ecological capacity» we mean nature's capability to produce resources and absorb waste. The percentage used is adjusted for trade. In other words, exporting ecological capacity in the form of goods and services would be subtracted from the country's use of nature (or ecological footprint), while import of ecological capacity would be added to their use of nature (or footprint). Among the countries that could not maintain their present GDP are all the «heavyweights» (see figures 4 and 5). India would need to cut its GDP by nearly half to live within its sustainable ecological capacity, while Colombia might theoretically still be able to double its GDP according to its ecological remainder.

If the GDP sustainability rate is above 100 percent, the ecological capacity of that country will support economic expansion. Whether such an expansion is a wise choice is another question, as we will discuss below. As long as the GDP sustainability rate, however, is below 100 percent, the country will be forced either to deplete its own natural capital or to procure the remainder of the ecological capacity needed to generate the gross domestic product by using the eco-capacity of other countries.

Assuming that, in spite of international economic competition, the creditor countries demand ever higher prices for the access to their ecological capacity, the debtor countries will be weakened as a result of rising cost. The creditor countries, on the other hand, will be strengthened. This mechanism will have the most severe consequences for low-income countries that already have a low sustainability rate, cause a large footprint per unit of gross domestic product, and are not competitive. In combination with a large population, this situation could be socially destabilising – and potentially explosive. All these factors apply to India, for instance, and to quite an extent also to China. At present, more than half of the world's population finds itself in this pressing situation.

The economically powerful nations will hardly be on the losing side in this struggle for a piece of the cake. In their fight for the additional capacity they need to maintain their income level, they have enough power to get what they want. For instance, the U.S.A. succeeded in demanding at Kyoto that virtually all industrialised countries lower the emission of greenhouse gases by the same percentage (approximately 8 percent by the year 2000). The U.S.A. will have to pay hardly anything for this undertaking, but other countries that already have much better environmental records must invest a great deal more for every percent of improvement.[14] Rich countries may be able to afford this; poor countries may have problems with it. If the Kyoto agreement is put into practice, the biggest debtor will gain in competitiveness over the others. Environmental policy becomes the power instrument of economic policy. If the social aspects of sustainability are also taken into account, this power play could trigger counterbalancing movements in the form of migration streams.

Ranking the Nations

In keeping with our original hypothesis, we postulate that ecological debtors – whether the debt is a function of their ecological capacity, their large per capita ecological footprint, or their large populations – will be less competitive[15] in the future than countries that do not live beyond their means. We also predict that profligate countries will be economically inferior to thrifty and efficient countries.

Ecological "Bulls" and "Bears"

If we look at today's competitive situation, we can distinguish four different starting points
(Figure 7):

- Green bulls
- Green bears
- Red bulls
- Red bears

As previously mentioned, the animals "bull" and "bear" were chosen by analogy to the terminology used in the financial markets, where "bulls" describe markets with rising prices or those in which market traders expect prices to rise. This is why we label competitive countries as bulls. The term "bears" stands for markets with dropping prices or those in which traders expect a drop in prices. Hence, we call noncompetitive countries bears.

Figure 7: Ecological Capacity and Competitiveness

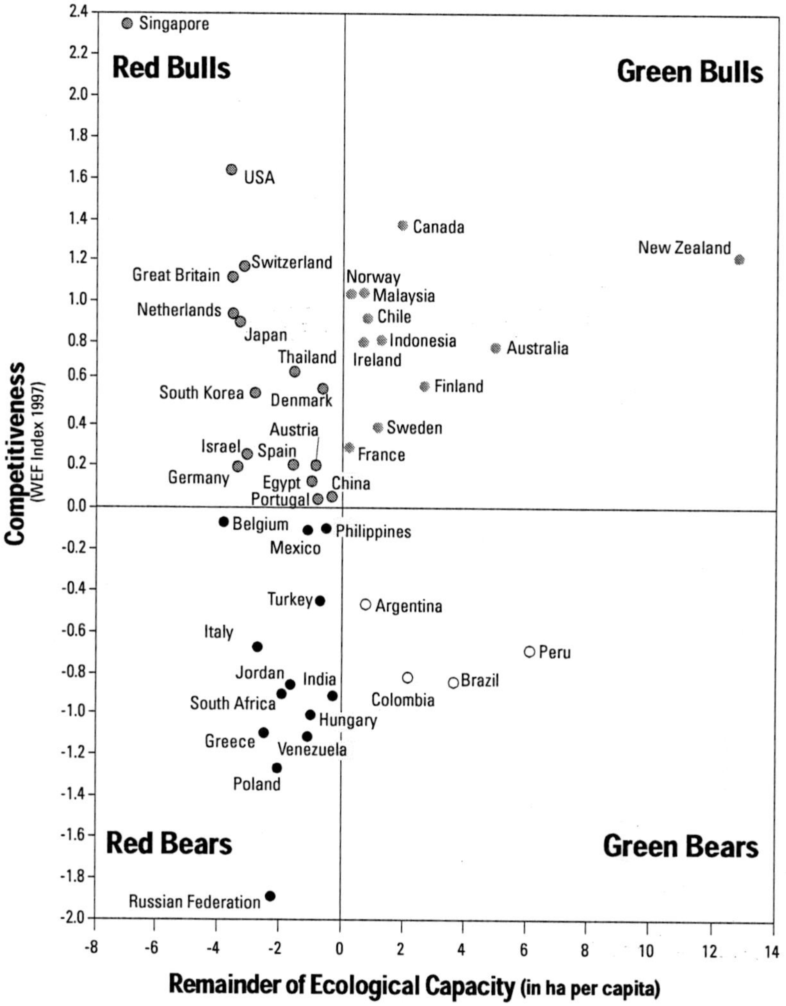

Red Bulls

Green Bulls

Singapore

USA

Canada

New Zealand

Switzerland
Great Britain
Norway
Malaysia
Netherlands
Chile
Japan
Indonesia   Australia
Thailand Ireland
South Korea   Denmark
Finland
Austria
Sweden
Israel Spain
France
Germany   Egypt   China
Portugal

Belgium   ● Philippines
Mexico

Turkey   O Argentina

Italy

O Peru

Jordan   India
O   O Brazil
South Africa   Colombia
Hungary
Greece
Venezuela
Poland

Red Bears

Green Bears

Russian Federation

Competitiveness (WEF Index 1997)

2.4, 2.2, 2.0, 1.8, 1.6, 1.4, 1.2, 1.0, 0.8, 0.6, 0.4, 0.2, 0.0, -0.2, -0.4, -0.6, -0.8, -1.0, -1.2, -1.4, -1.6, -1.8, -2.0

-8 -6 -4 -2 0 2 4 6 8 10 12 14

Remainder of Ecological Capacity (in ha per capita)

«Green» means that the country is an ecological creditor, «red» that it is an ecological debtor. The interesting fact is that there are only a few green bears — that is, countries that are ecologically well endowed, but who lack economic competitiveness. Most of them suffer from violent internal conflicts. The red bulls profit from historical advantages and are able to access ecological capacity abroad thanks to their accumulated financial resources. An intriguing case is Singapore. This country represents an interesting singularity: While the most competitive country of the study, it is also the one with the largest ecological deficit per person. However, with increasing ecological scarcity worldwide, the tide could turn, particularly for the ecological debtors.

Green Bulls

Competitive ecological creditors are either high-income countries with low population density, such as Canada, Australia, and Sweden, or semi-densely populated low-income countries, such as Indonesia and Malaysia. Due to their lower income levels, the latter have not used their ecological capacity to the full. Also, some of their remaining ecological capacity may be imaginary since tropical forests and agriculture are less likely than temperate counterparts to maintain initial yields. Exploiting the existing ecological reserves could have been (or still may be) a strategy for enhancing one's competitiveness. Maintaining or even improving one's competitive position today at the expense of future generations may, on the surface, appear a simple and politically attractive strategy, but it leads to the continuous deterioration of a once strong position. Destroying capital instead of protecting it and failing to realise the potential productivity of one's capital lead a business to bankruptcy in a market economy. We believe that this is true not only for businesses, but also for nations.

As economic growth is maintained, it must therefore be assumed that most of these countries will eventually become debtors. Canada, Finland, Australia, and New Zealand may be the last nations to become debtors, but they will inevitably reach that state too. The active management of their own footprints and of the existing ecological reserves may become the essential strategic capital of these nations, which they may then seek to maintain for the sake of their own competitiveness. If they succeed, they may well be among the winners of future competition.

Green Bears

Endowed with huge natural reserves, but nevertheless noncompetitive, are only four countries included in the study: Peru, Brazil, Colombia, and Argentina. The green bear position is the rarest and, with the exception of Argentina, includes only countries with major and mostly violent internal conflicts. Argentina, though, may still be suffering from the social debt of the military dictatorship that lasted until the late 1980s. Presently, they have a strong incentive to enhance their competitiveness in the short term through cheap exports and thus conceal internal political, social, and economic problems. They would do this by expanding their use of the existing ecological capacity and by largely externalising the environmental cost this entails. In terms of development policy, the strategy of the green bears is counterproductive in two respects: First, these countries squander their ecological capacity reserves and so jeopardise their future development and yield potential; second, besides their own economy, they also subsidise the economies of their trading partners, since most of the environmental costs cannot be passed on through prices.

As far as future competitiveness is concerned, the countries in this group are therefore bound to be among the losers.

Red Bulls

The majority of western industrial nations and some of the "tiger" states in Asia and China consume more natural resources than are available to them within their territories. Today, they are nevertheless internationally competitive.

As far as the western industrialised nations are concerned, this high degree of competitiveness is largely a result of the financial or real capital built up during the past – when ecological resources were abundant. Without belittling these achievements, one is tempted to suggest that they may have to reconsider this strategy in view of the ecological debtor's position into which they have manoeuvred themselves. After all, this situation poses no threat to the prosperity of these countries only as long as their strong competitive position allows them access to the ecological capacities outside their own countries – for a price which covers only part of the environmental costs incurred by the exporting countries.

The economic dependence of these countries on ecological creditors will invariably increase. The future competitiveness in this group may therefore depend to a large extent on how efficiently these countries generate their wealth. This issue will be addressed below in greater detail.

Red Bears

Compared with other nations, these countries face the most daunting challenge: They are not competitive, they have to rely on buying ecological capacity (or depleting their own assets), and most of these countries live at a relatively low level of prosperity. This category includes the countries of the once centrally planned and relatively closed economies of the former Eastern Bloc, as well as India, Belgium, Turkey, and Italy.

The current loose connection between ecological capacity and competitiveness may become tighter: We may safely assume that the ecological debtor nations, especially the "red bears," will encounter enormous problems in the future as they attempt to procure the required additional ecological capacity from the international markets. They simply will not have the economic power. If these countries fail in their efforts to massively enhance their eco-efficiency, they will be among the losers in the future competition. The resulting social conflicts will most likely generate social upheavals and large-scale migration to other countries – in particular to the geographic neighbours and to the prosperous states.

Conclusion

Looking at the relationship between the use of capacity and economic performance, we can conclude that today there is no clear-cut and uniform connection between competitiveness and the extent of over- or underuse of one's own ecological capacity. Still, it seems that countries with ecological remainders are more likely to remain competitive, particularly if they are not weakened by internal social conflicts. Also, it is quite possible that all those red bull countries would be less competitive were it not for the head start they have had since at least the beginning of this century. Without this historical advantage, it is questionable whether they would have been able to build competitive economies in today's ecologically constrained world.

Eco-Efficiency Leaders and Laggards

So far, we have only marginally touched on one of the central issues of our topic: the level of wealth. If ecological services become an essential cost factor in the twenty-first century, then it is not only the footprint – per land and per person – but also the related economic performance that will play a central role. Eco-efficiency, the link between footprint and economic performance, shows how many hectares a nation needs to generate its wealth.

For lack of a better prosperity indicator, we rely here on the gross domestic product. This unit accounts for the purchasing power in each country, but because it only reflects material wealth it is controversial (rightly so, we believe) from the ecological perspective. This is not the forum to engage in a discussion of the value of material wealth as a social and personal pursuit (although a significant portion of the people in the world would probably argue that more material wealth is indeed a worthwhile objective). Rather, our goal is to describe the relationship between gross domestic product and footprint.

The average eco-efficiency of the countries analysed is 0.47 hectares per 1,000 purchasing-power-adjusted U.S. dollars (0.47 ha/ 1,000 USD). If we divide the countries along this line of average eco-efficiency, two groups emerge (Figure 8):

- Eco-efficiency leaders
- Eco-efficiency laggards

Figure 8: Eco-Efficiency Leaders and Laggards

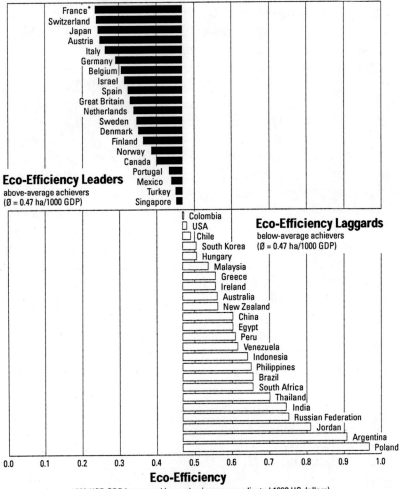

Eco-Efficiency
ha per 1000 USD GDP (measured in purchasing-power-adjusted 1993 US dollars)

The countries analysed require on average 0.47 hectares of bioproductive space to produce 1000 U.S. dollars (expressed in purchasing-power-adjusted U.S. dollars). This represents the amount of a country's currency required to buy a defined set of goods and services in the domestic market that would cost USD1000 in the United States. The analysis shows that Poland requires the largest area per purchasing-power-adjusted dollar — about double the world average. In other words, the country operates with low eco-efficiency. Therefore it leads the «eco-efficiency laggards». On the other hand, France, Switzerland, Japan, and Austria perform at the highest eco-efficiency levels and are therefore the «eco-efficiency leaders».

*Note: France, with its high dependence on nuclear power, which the footprint calculation does not address adequately, should make us interpret these results with some caution.

This analysis indicates that almost every highly industrialised country has a high degree of eco-efficiency and may count among the efficiency leaders. Again, one of the rather inglorious exceptions is the U.S.A. With respect to eco-efficiency, the United States trails far behind the other industrialised nations and finds itself in the company of eco-efficiency laggards such as Colombia and Chile. Three other countries with a large absolute share in the world's footprint, the heavyweights China, India, and Russia, also have a far below average eco-efficiency. These four countries, above all, must massively enhance their eco-efficiency. But this can only be done through technological and structural advancements and strategic investment – unless, of course, they buy access to more ecological capacity by fair means or foul play. Fair means require financial power and create winners and losers (who may well resist such moves on the grounds that they export jobs, an argument whose effectiveness is not improving by repetition); foul play could result in political, economic, social, and ultimately even military confrontation. First signs that some nations incline towards military solutions have emerged over the last decades, and not only in the battles in the Near East over water and oil. The former Yugoslavia, the former Soviet Union, central Africa, and the Indian subcontinent offer frightening examples.

Things look even bleaker if the hurdle for the eco-efficiency leaders is set a bit higher. If, instead of the average eco-efficiency existing today, we take as benchmark the degree of efficiency that would be necessary for sustained and sustainable worldwide operations, we find that only 13 countries meet this standard. With increasing material wealth and worldwide population growth, this benchmark must naturally be raised a great deal higher, with the effect that no country is likely to meet it.

Even assuming, for instance, that all the people in the world lived economically and ecologically on the same level as the eco-efficiency leader Switzerland, the world population as a whole would still live beyond its means by of factor of two. If our yardstick were the U.S.A., the country with the biggest footprint per person, we would exceed the capacity by a factor of five. If we took India as the standard, the country with the smallest footprint (and a low income level), we would still have doubled our capacity. As we said above, this makes the expected doubling of the world population appear in a different light.

This analysis shows quite starkly that no country is really ready for the future and that none may serve as a model or benchmark. But the rich, eco-efficient countries could at least lead the way to the general direction: producing the same with less. Eco-efficiency must – and will – be the central factor of the future, the determinant of failure or success. But it must not be misunderstood: Eco-efficiency may be a contingent condition for future sustainability, but taken on its own it is not the only, or even a sufficient condition. Changes in the consumer habits of the big feet nations as well as the stabilisation of the world population are equally indispensable.

One remarkable outcome of this analysis is that highly developed and relatively prosperous countries with low ecological capacity, such as Switzerland or Germany, have a high eco-efficiency, whereas countries with large reserves such as Australia and New Zealand, come off relatively badly. In this case necessity or, more precisely, a comparatively high ecological scarcity, seems to be the mother of invention. However, innovation requires investment, which is not easily afforded by poorer countries.

In our initial considerations we assumed that the thrifty would outrun the profligate in a market economy in the same way as those with reserves will outrun those without reserves, once the environment turns into a scarce commodity and hence into a cost factor. To investigate this in more detail, we developed a series of sustainability comparisons based on analysis of 44 nations according to various combinations of factors. These factors are eco-capacity and ecological deficit, eco-efficiency, and competitiveness.

Eco-Efficiency and Ecological Capacity: Green and Red Leaders and Laggards

By juxtaposing the ecological footprint and the eco-efficiency findings, we distinguish four different levels of development among the countries analysed (Figure 9):

- Green Efficiency Leaders
- Red Efficiency Leaders
- Green Efficiency Laggards
- Red Efficiency Laggards.

How do these four categories differ, and which opportunities and risks are inherent in these positions?

Figure 9: Eco-Efficiency and Ecological Capacity

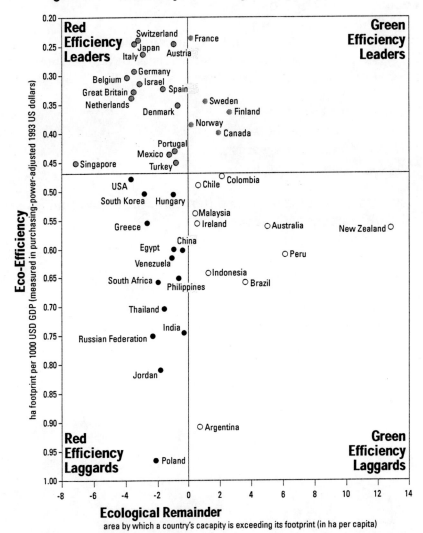

Eco-Efficiency

ha footprint per 1000 USD GDP (measured in purchasing-power-adjusted 1993 US dollars)

Ecological Remainder

area by which a country's cacapity is exceeding its footprint (in ha per capita)

Once we combine the eco-efficiency analysis with the footprint analysis, it shows that the rich and highly industrialised countries that have lower capacity per capita are performing at higher eco-efficiency levels. Examples are Switzerland, Japan, Austria, and Germany. On the other hand, lower-income countries, and particularly those with more outdated production systems, rate lower in eco-efficiency.

Green Efficiency Leaders

These countries, the most progressive in terms of sustainability, live below their capacity, and they do so very efficiently. Besides the Scandinavian countries, Canada and France[16] also fall into this category. They are in the best possible starting position both to compete economically and to meet future ecological challenges. But all these countries run the risk of becoming ecological debtors if they fail to enhance their eco-efficiency to compensate for their growing footprint, which is increasing due to economic growth or population growth.

Red Efficiency Leaders

These countries already live above their capacity, but they do so very efficiently. In this category we find mainly the countries of the EU, Singapore, and Japan. To get out of their ecological debt and maintain their future economic position, these countries must decrease their footprint even further in relation to their wealth. Given the efficiency level they have already reached, this might turn out to be difficult in the long run, due to the decreasing marginal benefits (see endnote 15). But these countries are nevertheless in a good competitive starting position: Because they have already embarked successfully on the structural changes and investments necessary for high eco-efficiency, they will need to make fewer economic adjustments than the eco-efficiency laggards.

Green Efficiency Laggards

These countries live below their capacity, and they do so inefficiently. For more prosperous countries such as Australia, New Zealand, or Ireland, improving this situation may not pose a great economic challenge. They simply lack the economic and ecological incentives to operate more efficiently.

This situation is more serious for countries at a lower level of economic development, such as the Asian group, including Indonesia and Malaysia, as well as for the Latin American countries, including Colombia, Chile, Peru, Brazil, and Argentina. In their case, increasing economic activity is unlikely to go hand in hand with a proportionally enhanced eco-efficiency: Money and know-how are not readily available, and the competitive pressure exerted by the international community will force these countries to exploit their existing, but dwindling, reserves for the sake of material wealth. The short-term prospects for these countries are good, but in the medium and long term, their low efficiency and dwindling or exhausted ecological remainders will weaken their economic standing.

Red Efficiency Laggards

These countries, the most backward in terms of sustainability, live above their capacity, and they do so very inefficiently. The most prominent and problematic among these is the U.S.A. The future competitiveness of these countries will depend to a large degree on the current level of economic development, and on their financial and technological potential. Supported by its great political and military power, the U.S.A. may be the only such country where these factors will be conducive to improving the competitive position. Compared with the other three groups of countries, these countries will most likely be on the losing side.

Eco-Efficiency and Competitiveness: Efficient and Inefficient Bulls and Bears

Our analysis so far has shown that a nation's ecological footprint and its eco-efficiency do not yet have the final word on the competitiveness of a country. In fact, there are still a few countries like the United States that live inefficiently, on a big footprint and beyond their means, with little apparent adverse effect on their competitiveness at the moment. But, as we have argued, there are good reasons to expect that this will change in the future (Figure 10).

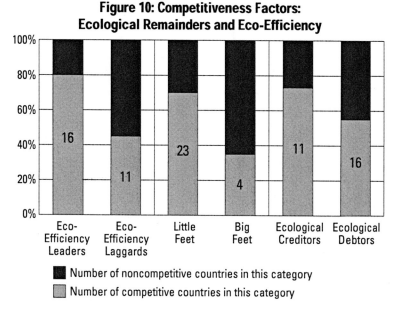

**Figure 10: Competitiveness Factors:
Ecological Remainders and Eco-Efficiency**

■ Number of noncompetitive countries in this category

▨ Number of competitive countries in this category

Of the 20 eco-efficiency leaders, only 4 (or one-fifth) have a competitiveness lower than the average. Among the 24 laggards, 13 (or over half) fall into this category. These figures seem to point towards synergy between eco-efficiency and competitiveness. Similar observations can be made about the other categories. The least interesting one is the middle one: Rich countries tend to have larger footprints and are more likely to be competitive. The most interesting trend is that debtors seem to find it harder than creditors to be competitive. Obviously, this analysis is not based on a sample size that would provide statistically significant results. This analysis just shows possible connections that need to be analysed in more detail on a country by country basis.

What is striking, however, is that 16 of the 20 eco-efficiency leaders (about 80 percent), but only 11 of the 24 eco-efficiency laggards (about 45 percent) are competitive. This can be interpreted in two ways: Either eco-efficiency already offers a competitive edge, or competitiveness and high eco-efficiency are not mutually exclusive. This is even clearer in the case of the big feet and the little feet, and in that of the ecological debtors and creditors. The current impact of these aspects of ecological performance on competitiveness is still weak and not as clearly present as in the case of eco-efficiency. (However, as discussed, there are many good reasons to expect the influence of the other impacts to become far stronger in the future.)

One possible reason why these correlations, though existent, are still relatively weak may be that it does not yet matter so much today in financial terms whether a country lives beyond its means or not, whether it has a big or a small footprint, and whether it is efficient or inefficient. As long as the environment has no price tag and externalising costs is still encouraged through present regimes of globalisation, things are unlikely to change radically. This status quo is effectively consolidated by a number of factors: the deregulation and liberalisation of world trade, the resulting rivalry, and the concurrent power drift away from governments. This allows ecological debtors to continue dodging the conversion of this ecological (and interest-free) debt into monetary liabilities.

It is to be expected that countries with low eco-efficiency will get the roughest deal in future competition. This can also be seen in our analysis of the relationship between competitiveness and eco-efficiency (Figure 11).

Among the inefficient bears and inefficient bulls are mainly those countries that used to be labelled "developing" or "newly industrialised" countries, but also the U.S.A. (Figure 11). Those countries within these two groups that are highly competitive today and that have a high level of prosperity will have better chances of raising their efficiency to a sustainable level. These include the U.S.A. and the two countries with ecological reserves, Australia and New Zealand. The analysis also shows that the European countries, including the EU, Switzerland, Norway, as well as Singapore and Japan are clearly better prepared to meet the challenges of the future than the rest of the world. Relatively strict environmental laws and an ecologically demanding market appear to drive these countries towards the higher degree of efficiency and innovation that is plainly conducive to better competitive standing.

Figure 11: Eco-Efficiency and Competitiveness

Eco-Efficiency (ha footprint per 1000 USD GDP (measured in purchasing-power-adjusted 1993 US dollars))

Competitiveness (WEF Index 1997)

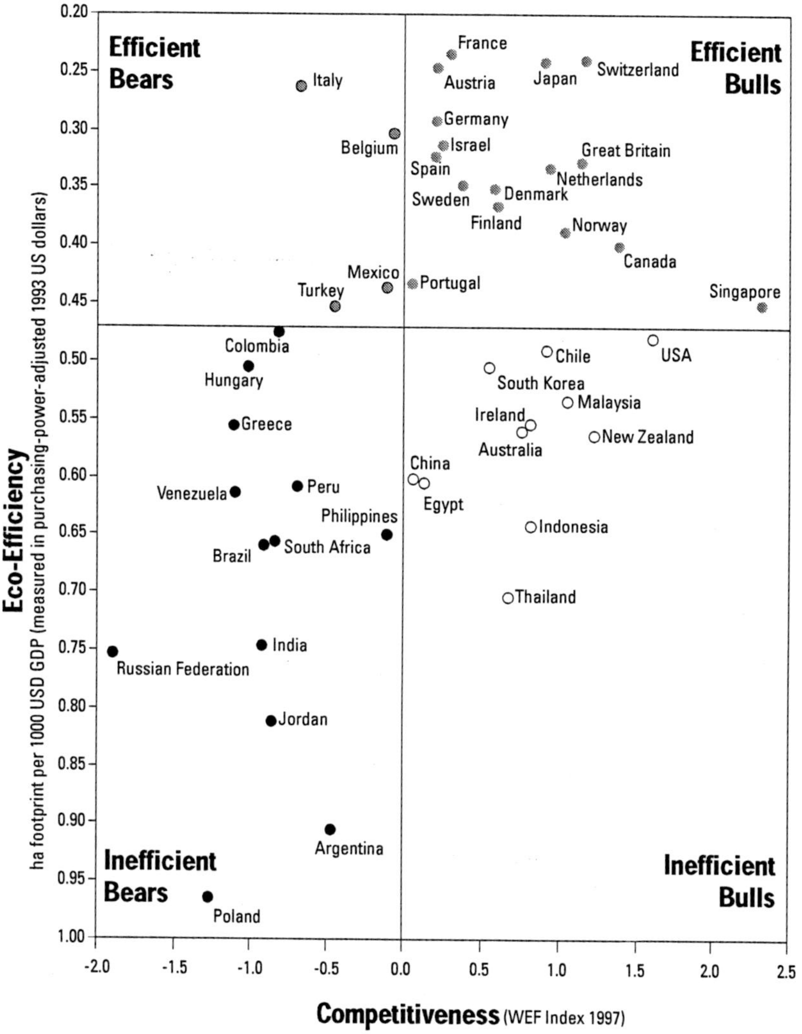

Of the eco-efficiency leaders, only 4 (or one-fifth) are not competitive (Italy, Belgium, Mexico, and Turkey). This shows that even today, eco-efficiency and competitiveness are not, as sometimes assumed, at cross-purposes (see also figure 10).

A process can rightly be called eco-efficient only if it both reduces the environmental burden and creates economic value. The European countries, Japan, and Singapore seem to be best at reconciling these two factors. The remaining countries still have these changes ahead of them, which will cost them time and money and potentially damage their position in the competitive race. This strongly suggests that the efficient bulls must do everything in their power to come to strict international environmental agreements that are as cost-effective as possible. The fact that the environment would then have a (higher) price for these countries does not invalidate this argument, because competition involves advantages and disadvantages only in relative terms. If we succeeded in putting a price on the environment, the efficient bulls would lead the competitive race – the others would be able to narrow this lead only by investing a great deal of time, money, and knowledge. But it must be kept in mind that the world as a whole is already in ecological debt today, and that many efficient bulls also live above their capacity.

The situation in which the efficient bears find themselves varies somewhat by country. Both Belgium and Italy have a high level of prosperity, are embedded in a larger economic structure, and are unlikely to enhance their competitiveness at the expense of environmental performance. This means that, in the medium term, they may be among the winners. The situation looks different for Turkey and Mexico: The relatively low level of prosperity, lack of technical skills, and restricted access to financial markets make it difficult for them to restructure their economies towards eco-efficiency. Also, as these countries continue to grow economically, they are likely to slip even further into ecological debt.

The inefficient bears will have to rely on technology transfer as well as on economic and financial co-operation if they want to see ecological and economic improvements. Since only the EU and Japan are highly eco-efficient and have built up corresponding knowledge, their co-operation with inefficient bears is paramount to world sustainability. It goes without saying that such a co-operation can be beneficial for both sides (new markets develop, for instance). The U.S.A., with its recent push for "trade, not development aid," may well run into difficulties here because its consumer behaviour, its products, and its production methods hardly qualify as being eco-efficient.

Winners and Losers in Competition

As we have argued throughout the study, the countries on the losing side in the future competition will be those that
1. live above their ecological capacity,
2. use ecological services too lavishly in relation to their prosperity, and
3. host individuals who use a disproportionately large amount of ecological services in their consumer behaviour and consumption level.

We also hold that, the more of these weak points a country has, the greater this competitive disadvantage.
If we delve somewhat deeper into the previous analyses, we also see the following patterns:
- Countries with a large footprint per person (big feet) and a low income level have a worse starting position than little feet that are also on a low income level.
- Countries with a large footprint per person (big feet) and a high income level have a better starting position than big feet on a low income level.
- Countries with a small footprint per person (little feet) and a high income level have a better starting position than little feet on a low income level.
- The impact of environmental scarcity will be less negative for eco-efficient debtors than for inefficient debtors.
- A high level of competitiveness today will make it easier for a country to obtain missing ecological capacity and/or to enhance its eco-efficiency.

- A high income level today will make it easier for a country to obtain missing ecological capacity and/or to enhance its eco-efficiency.
- A low income level today increases the social and political pressure to overuse the environment at the expense of others.

If we use these features to compare all the countries, we can distinguish the winners and losers of the competition of the future. Table 1 lists the winners and Table 2 the potential losers, both assessed in terms of their future competitiveness.

Table 1: The Potential Winners in Future Global Competition[17]

Country	Future competitiveness	Eco-efficiency index	Ecological remainders index	Relative footprint Index	Relative standard of living index		Present competitiveness	
Eco-Efficiency Leader / Creditor / Little Feet								
no country								
Eco-Efficiency Leader / Creditor / Big Feet								
France*	△ ▽	100	36	65	very high	80	✓	0.30
Sweden	△	85	41	46	high	78	✓	0.38
Finland	△	82	49	45	high	75	✓	0.60
Norway	△	79	36	43	high	73	✓	1.04
Canada	△	77	45	27	very high	89	✓	1.38
Eco-Efficiency Leader / Debtor / Big Feet								
Switzerland	▽	99	20	56	very high	97	✓	1.17
Japan	▽	99	19	63	very high	81	✓	0.91
Austria	▽	98	31	65	high	76	✓	0.20
Italy	▽ ▷	96	21	64	high	73		-0.68
Germany	▽	92	19	53	very high	4	✓	0.20
Belgium	▽ ▷	90	17	56	high	75		-0.07
Great Britain	▽	87	18	54	high	72	✓	1.14
Netherlands	▽	86	18	53	high	72	✓	0.93
Denmark	▽	84	32	46	high	77	✓	0.58
Singapore	▽	70	0	33	high	73	✓	2.23
Israel	▽ ▷	89	20	73	medium	48	✓	0.24
Spain	▽ ▷	88	28	68	medium	52	✓	0.20
Portugal	▷ ◁	73	31	68	low	38	✓	0.05
Eco-Efficiency Leader / Debtor / Little Feet								
Mexico	▷	72	30	81	low	24		-0.11
Turkey	▷ ◁	71	32	86	very low	18		-0.45

*Note: France, with its high dependence on nuclear power, which the footprint calculation does not address adequately, should make us interpret these results with some caution.[17]

Future competitiveness: △ potentially higher, ▽ potentially lower, countries printed in brighter letters are candidates for moving up or down one category.

Countries who are already eco-efficient today are more likely to be among the winners of the future global competition — particularly if they still have not become ecological debtors. The table shows the future competitiveness of nations in descending order.

Table 2: The Potential Losers in Future Global Competition[17]

Country	Future competitiveness	Eco-efficiency index	Ecological remainders index	Relative footprint index	Relative standard of living index		Present competitiveness
Eco-Efficiency Laggard / Creditor / Big Feet							
Ireland	▷◁	56	39	46	medium	47	✓ 0.81
Australia	▷◁	56	61	14	high	74	✓ 0.78
New Zealand	▷◁	55	100	28	high	61	✓ 1.22
Malaysia	▷△	59	38	74	low	25	✓ 1.04
Brazil	▷△	42	54	76	very low	18	-0.84
Argentina	▷△	8	39	67	very low	16	-0.48
Eco-Efficiency Laggard / Creditor / Little Feet							
Chile	▷◁	65	39	82	low	20	✓ 0.92
Colombia	▷△	68	46	87	very low	16	-0.81
Peru	▷△	49	66	92	very low	8	-0.69
Indonesia	▷△	44	42	94	very low	5	✓ 0.82
Eco-Efficiency Laggard / Debtor / Big Feet							
USA	◁▷	67	18	0	very high	100	✓ 1.61
Russian Fed.	△	29	24	45	high	34	-1.89
South Korea	△	63	21	73	low	28	✓ 0.54
Hungary	△	63	31	76	low	25	-1.01
Greece	△	56	23	65	low	31	-1.10
Venezuela	△	48	30	68	low	25	✓ 0.11
Poland	△▽	0	25	65	very low	16	-1.27
South Africa	△▽	42	26	75	very low	19	-0.89
Thailand	△▽	36	28	79	very low	14	✓ 0.67
Eco-Efficiency Laggard / Debtor / Little Feet							
China	△▽	50	34	69	very low	5	✓ 0.06
Egypt	△▽	50	31	96	very low	4	✓ 0.11
Philippines	▽	43	33	93	very low	6	-0.11
India	▽	30	34	100	very low	0	-0.92
Jordan	▽	22	27	88	very low	6	-0.85

Future competitiveness: △ potentially higher, ▽ potentially lower, countries printed in brighter letters are candidates for moving up or down one category.

Countries that perform with low eco-efficiency today will more likely be among the losers of the future global competition. If they still have an ecological remainder (i.e., they are ecological creditors), they stand better chances, particularly if their current standard of living is not too low.

Outlook: Environmental Strategies at the Turn of the Millennium

Our analysis of the winners and losers in future competition presents the starting points at which various countries find themselves on the threshold to the next millennium. But the present position held by each country can not and must not be taken for granted. On the contrary, it offers a basis for change: for creating and re-orienting sustainability strategies whose global perspective can be applied locally whether in a unilateral or multi-lateral fashion. This strategic re-orientation of environmental policy must take into account the available capacity that is predefined by the limited ecologically productive area of this planet.

The implementation of this principle must be approached from two sides: on the supply side by effective management of the ecological capacity, and on the demand side by efficient use of ecological services delivered by natural capital. Specifically, we arrive at the following conclusions and recommendations:

Supply-side management
The minimum requirement for sustainability is the maintenance of ecological capacity; enhancing it is even better. This may be achieved by:
1. upgrading and/or enlarging the bio-productive area;
2. containing the destruction of bio-productive areas by combating the spread of deserts, soil erosion, soil compacting, or overbuilding.

Demand-side management
Our footprint will have to shrink overall. This can be achieved in three ways, by:
1. lowering global population (particularly in the industrialised countries with their high per capita footprints);
2. lowering consumption level;
3. increasing eco-efficiency in both production (moving away from production technologies with large footprint) and consumption

of commodities (changing the mix of commodities consumed by households, moving away from consumption patterns that produce larger footprints).

The supply-oriented strategies for maintaining and enlarging ecological capacity affect mainly agriculture, forestry and fisheries, and municipal and regional planning. However, many of the agricultural, forestry, and fishery initiatives will require international agreements and co-ordinated implementation. Otherwise, there is the risk that some countries may take advantage of the self-restraint of others, or inversely that "free riders" will invalidate the efforts. The deregulation of the markets within the GATT free-trade agreement sets the bar for such agreements even higher. Since international consent is normally reached only in the face of extremely pressing and immediate problems, this long-term strategy, in spite of its significance, may face many obstacles and delays. The sustainable management of municipalities and regions can be implemented more rapidly and directly at the local level.

But demand-oriented strategies are also fraught with some virtually insuperable problems. Efforts to reduce the population or the population growth rate often meet with ethical, moral, and social objections.

The other option – that of universally lowering consumption and production levels – is a rather unlikely scenario in the medium term, considering widespread global poverty and the reluctance of rich nations to lower their living standards voluntarily.

These circumstances underscore the importance of the eco-efficiency option. But even this strategy will be difficult to implement smoothly. This is where the eco-efficient red bulls play a central role. To maintain their position, these countries must reduce their ecological deficits by further enhancing their eco-efficiency, or by continuing to use some of the ecological capacity of other countries. One can only conjecture how long it will take before the ecological creditors receive commensurate payments, or how long it will take before they become aware of their own strategic reserves and use this power base to further their own economies. Granting the possibility of this compensation scenario, it is already advisable today to help inefficient countries raise their efficiency levels, whether these are countries with ecological remainders (creditors) or with eco-deficits (debtors). Such help would include the transfer of technology and expertise, the bilateral implementation of common objectives (joint imple-mentation), and other forms of economic and ecological co-operation.

Although an eco-efficiency strategy can, in principle, be implemented without changing the economic parameters, this approach has a number of inherent economic and ecological risks. Since gains in eco-efficiency normally mean progress in productivity, both supply of and demand for products and services will rise. The quantity effects triggered by this normally outweigh any improvements in eco-efficiency. In such a situation the relative footprint (i.e., the ecological footprint required to generate one unit of the gross domestic product) would become smaller, but the country's absolute footprint would grow bigger. The increasing footprint would be aggravated by population growth. Since the earth's ecological capacity is limited, overall growth of humanity's ecological demands, whether through increased population or higher per capita consumption, must be prevented.

The only economically efficient and ecologically effective strategy available today to prevent this from happening is introducing free-market economic instruments into environmental policy. These control the demand for ecological capacity by including external environmental costs either through revenue-neutral interventions (e.g., levied energy or carbon fees where the generated income is reimbursed to the citizen or CO_2 emission certificates) or less favourable income-generating regulations (e.g., environmental taxes). Introducing such instruments offers one decisive advantage: When the ecological accuracy inherent in the price promotes the innovation required to enhance the supply- and demand-side eco-efficiency, financial, human, and natural resources are deployed in the best possible economic way. This prevents economic inefficiencies, enhances economic performance, and potentially increases income.[18]

A Tool for the Sustainability Debate

Sustainability demands that all can secure their quality of life, while at the same time humanity's footprint is reduced. Impossible? No! Three mutually complementary strategies can help us reduce our footprint without jeopardising our quality of life.

We can:
- enhance nature's bio-productivity in a sustainable manner. The yields and services of nature can be increased without diminishing the natural capital. This can be achieved by increasing the bioproductive surface area or by increasing the health of the ecosystems on existing areas. Examples include permaculture, terraces on mountain slopes to prevent erosion, careful irrigation projects that preserve the fertility of the soil and use water sustainably, reforestation, afforestation, and the use of solar energy on otherwise unutilised rooftops.
- make better use of the harvested resources. We can produce the same output with a smaller input. Examples include low-power light bulbs, heat pumps, district heating power stations, acclimatised buildings, and recycling (see also the box on eco-efficiency on page 25).
- consume less by reducing populations or per capita consumption. We can live our lives lessening our dependence on cars and other wasteful products. At the same time we would save money and thus could afford more leisure time. This simpler life style would also put less stress on our health and give us more time to enjoy the quality of our lives.

To guarantee the success of these resource-conserving strategies, we must ensure that everybody involved is, in fact, more satisfied with life thanks to the chosen strategy. Otherwise, new strategies may not get the support they need – or could even backfire.

One possible solution to the problem of resource overuse and inefficiency contributing to natural capital scarcity lies in establishing tradable rights to defined amounts of ecological services. Assuming that everybody in the world has the same right to use nature's capacity, we could determine these rights in quantitative terms by taking the present average ecological footprint of 2.65 hectares per person as a reference point. We now issue rights in the shape of tradable certificates as proposed by the U.S.A. at the Kyoto World Conference on Climate, among others. This means that everybody would be allowed to use as much nature as they like; they would just have to buy additional rights from others for the part of their footprint that exceeded the average. Conversely, the rights accruing from below-average footprints could be sold. In specific terms this means that the "big feet" would need to buy a certain number of hectares of ecological capacity from the "little feet" that had and were willing to sell this quantity. This would entail more equally shared rights to the global commons for everyone and a money transfer from the "big feet" to the "little feet".

In terms of footprints, the situation would therefore not be fundamentally different from today's situation – but the creditor countries would be paid for their share of nature. Nevertheless, there would be an incentive for all to reduce their footprint: for the "little feet" in order to receive more transfer payments, and for the "big feet" countries to pay less for excess footprints.[19]

To illustrate this idea, let's put numbers to an example with extremely conservative assumptions: Let's put the value of an average bioproductive hectare of land at, say, 1,000 U.S. dollars, about USD 0.10 per square metre. If we reckon with an interest on capital of 5 percent, this would mean an annual lease rate of USD 50 per hectare, or half a cent per square metre. In the case of the U.S.A., this would mean that on average every inhabitant would buy the additional rights for about 8 hectares at a total price per year of USD 380. This sum is about one-third of the average annual income of a person in India. The United States as a whole would therefore have to spend about USD 103 billion per year for purchasing these rights, which corresponds to about 1.8 percent of the country's gross domestic product. The other "big feet" would also have to buy rights but would need to spend far less to support their smaller footprint per person. The money would go to those countries that sell these rights, that is, the "little feet" such as India, China, or Indonesia. India, for instance, would receive transfer payments of USD 90 billion, which is more than 8 percent of its gross domestic product (see Table 3 and Table 4).

Table 3: The Potential Transfers of Payments Tradable Permits Would Generate (for beneficiaries)

Sellers of ecological capacity (= beneficiaries of the payments)

Country	Payment per country (million USD)	Amount per capita (USD)	Percentage of GDP (purchasing-power-adjusted 1993 US dollars)
Chile	112	8	0.1%
Jordan	220	38	1.6%
Mexico	252	3	0.0%
Colombia	1'180	33	0.8%
Peru	1'299	53	2.0%
Turkey	1'774	28	0.6%
Philippines	4'053	58	2.5%
Egypt	4'751	73	3.7%
Indonesia	12'746	63	2.9%
India	89'838	**93**	**8.6%**
China	**90'548**	73	3.6%

▷ Assumption behind examples: see text
▷ Bold print: the maximum and minimum in each column

If China could have sold the services of its remaining capacity via tradable permits, it would have received over USD 90 billion (or USD 73 per person). This corresponds to 3.6 percent of their GDP.

Table 4: The Potential Transfers of Payments Tradable Permits Would Generate (for paying countries)

Buyers of ecological capacity

Country	Payment per country (million USD)	Amount per capita (USD)	Percentage of GDP (purchasing-power-adjusted 1993 US dollars)
USA	**-102'557**	**-382**	-1.8%
Russian Fed.	-24'505	-167	**-2.1%**
Germany	-10'837	-132	0.7%
Japan	-10'356	-82	-0.5%
Canada	-7'598	-252	-1.3%
Great Britain	-7'464	-127	-0.8%
Australia	-5'888	-317	-2.0%
Italy	-4'431	-77	-0.5%
France	-4'231	-72	-0.4%
Brazil	-3'743	-22	-0.5%
Poland	-2'789	-72	-1.7%
Spain	-2'281	-57	-0.5%
Argentina	-2'209	-62	-1.5%
Netherlands	-2'078	-132	-0.8%
South Korea	-1'716	-37	-0.6%
Sweden	-1'439	-162	-1.0%
Venezuela	-1'308	-57	-0.9%
Belgium	-1'194	-117	-0.7%
South Africa	-1'187	-27	-0.6%
New Zealand	-904	-247	-1.8%
Finland	-862	-167	-1.0%
Switzerland	-861	-117	-0.6%
Denmark	-844	-162	-1.0%
Norway	-776	-177	-1.1%
Greece	-761	-72	-1.0%
Malaysia	-681	-32	-0.5%
Singapore	-657	-227	-1.4%
Austria	-583	-72	-0.4%
Ireland	-581	-162	-1.5%
Portugal	-563	-57	-0.7%
Thailand	-445	-7	-0.2%
Hungary	-225	-22	-0.4%
Israel	-219	-37	-0.3%

▷ Assumption behind examples: see text
▷ Bold print: the maximum and minimum in each column

If Germany had compensated the world for the bioproductive area it used beyond its global eco-capacity share at the rate of half a cent per square meter each year (or USD 50 per hectare each year), its citizens would have paid USD 132 each for 1993. This corresponds to approximately USD 11 billion — or 0.7 percent of their GDP. The Russian Fedaration would need to spend 2 percent of its GDP to pay for its above average use of ecological capacity.

The argument that intervening in free-market forces is unnecessary because the scarcity of resources leads automatically to innovation is unsound for several reasons.[20] First, the prices that are supposed to reflect the scarcity of a commodity do not, in fact, reflect today's ecological scarcity and severely underrate the future scarcity. Second, innovative capability depends upon access to economic, ecological, and social resources. It is precisely of this capability that many countries have been historically deprived, whether through political colonialisation, or through persistent exploitation of resources through deregulated world trade accompanied by the externalisation of ecological and social cost. Necessity may be the mother of invention, but without capital and expertise no birth takes place. For this reason we cannot, and should not, leave the solution of the problem to the "invisible hand" of a free market without caps or ground rules. Instead, we should seize the power of market-based solutions for achieving socially determined goals, since such incentives are so effective.

To implement this co-operative eco-efficiency strategy, a global solution would certainly be preferable, but it is not a prerequisite for addressing the challenge. We believe that, even without such agreements, nations' self-interest encourages improvements in ecological performance. Obviously, with more advanced international agreements and corresponding institutional support, the incentives for implementing ecologically superior performance would be greater and come more rapidly. But even without such international agreements, countries can still develop bilateral agreements on co-operating within an eco-efficiency programme. The fact that the eco-inefficient country, through enhancing its own eco-efficiency, becomes more competitive and prosperous, serves the interest of the eco-efficient partner, because successful economic co-operation with competitive partners also promotes one's own competitiveness. Both sides should therefore derive economic benefit. For this wealth-enhancing eco-efficiency revolution to proceed as efficiently and effectively as possible, the use of free-market environmental policy instruments, such as a revenue-neutral tax reform (moving from taxing income to taxing the use of ecological services) or emission certificates, must be encouraged.[21]

An eco-efficiency revolution is not only desirable, it is indispensable for enhancing competitiveness. There are sufficient indicators in this study to show that this thesis is already reality today. Nations who decide to stay clear of this revolution will soon be left behind. The choice is theirs.

References

Barnes, Peter (1999): Who'll Get the Manna When the Heavens Charge Rent? *The American Prospect,* Spring 1999.

Davidson, Gavin and Christina Robb (1994): The Ecological Footprint of the Lions Gate Bridge. School of Resource Management, Simon Fraser University, Burnaby, British Columbia, 1994.

Deumling, Diana, Ritik Dholakia, and Mathis Wackernagel (1999): Calculate Your Ecological Footprint: 13 Simple Questions Will Assess Your Use of Nature, Excel spreadsheet available from Redefining Progress, San Francisco through <*deumling@rprogress.org*>.

Ehrlich, Paul, Gary Wolff, Gretchen Daily, Jennifer B. Hughes, Scott Daily, Michael Dalton, Lawrence Goulder (1999): Knowledge and the Environment, *Ecological Economics,* Vol. 30, No 1 (pp. 267–284).

Hawken, Paul, Amory Lovins, and Hunter Lovins (1999): *Natural Capitalism.* New York: Little Brown.

Holmberg, John, Ulrika Lundqvist, Karl-Henrik Robèrt, and M. Wackernagel (1999): The Ecological Footprint from a Systems Perspective of Sustainability, *The International Journal of Sustainable Development and World Ecology,* Vol. 6 pp. 17–33.

Kautsky, Nils, H. Berg, Carl Folke, Jannson Larsson, and Max Troell (1997): Ecological Footprint for Assessment of Resource Use and Development Limitations in Shrimp and Tilapia Aquiculture, *Aquiculture Research,* No. 28, Vol. 10. Oct. pp. 753–766.

Motavalli, Jim (1999): Conversations with Dr. Nafis Sadik: The UN's Prescription for Family Planning, *E The Environmental Magazine,* July/August 1999, Vol. 10, No.4, pp. 10–13.

Myers, Norman and Julian L. Simon (1994): *Scarcity or Abundance? A Debate on the Environment.* New York: W.W. Norton & Co.

Noss, Reed F. and Allen Y. Cooperrider (1994): *Saving Nature's Legacy – Protecting and Restoring Biodiversity.* Washington DC: Island Press.

Rees, William E. and Mathis Wackernagel (1999): Monetary Analysis: Turning a Blind Eye on Sustainability, *Ecological Economics,* Vol. 29, No. 1. pp. 47–52.

Schaltegger, Stefan and Andreas Sturm (1989): Ökologieinduzier-te Entscheidungsinstrumente des Managements, WWZ-Discussion Paper No. 8914, Basel: WWZ.

Schaltegger, Stefan and Andreas Sturm (1990): Ökologische Rationalität, in: Die Unternehmung Nr. 4/90, S. 273–290.

Schmidheiny, Stefan (1992): *Changing Course*. Cambridge, MA: The MIT Press.

Sterner, Thomas, ed. (1999): *The Market and the Environment*. Cheltenham, UK: Edward Elgar.

UNCTAD/Ellipson (1998): Standardized Environmental Performance Indicators – Appropriate Indicators for Communicating Environmental Performance. Info via E-Mail: *contact@ellipson. com* or Fax: ++41-61-2619313.

van Vuuren, Detlef, E.M.W. Smeets, and H.A.M. de Kruijf (1999): The Ecological Footprint of Benin, Bhutan, Costa Rica and the Netherlands, RIVM report 807005004. Bilthoven, the Netherlands: National Institute of Public Health and the Environment (RIVM).

Wackernagel, Mathis (1998): The Ecological Footprint of Santiago de Chile, *Local Environment,* Vol.3, No.1 Feb 1998.

Wackernagel, Mathis and Dick Richardson (1998): How to Calculate a Household's Ecological Footprint, Xalapa: Anáhuac University of Xalapa, and Austin: University of Texas;

Wackernagel, Mathis, Larry Onisto, Alejandro Callejas Linares, Ina Susana López Falfán, Jesus Méndez García, Ana Isabel Suárez Guerrero, Ma. Guadalupe Suárez Guerrero (1997): *Ecological Footprints of Nations: How Much Nature Do They Use? How Much Nature Do They Have?* Commissioned by the Earth Council for the Rio+5 Forum. International Council for Local Environmental Initiatives, Toronto, 1997. (available from ICLEI: Fax +1-416-3921478, E-Mail: *iclei@iclei.org*, Price: 30 USD including disks with all tables and calculations for 1995). Also, the calculations for 1993 exist. New calculations with 1996 data are in preparation for WWF International and the Union de Banques Privées of Geneva.

Wackernagel, Mathis, Larry Onisto, Patricia Bello, Alejandro Callejas Linares, Ina Susana López Falfán, Jesus Méndez García,

Ana Isabel Suárez Guerrero, and Ma. Guadalupe Suárez Guerrero (1999a): National Natural Capital Accounting with the Ecological Footprint Concept, *Ecological Economics,* Vol. 29 No. 3 (June), pp. 375–390.

Wackernagel, Mathis, Lillemor Lewan, and Carina Hansson (1999b): Evaluating the Use of Natural Capital with the Ecological Footprint: Applications in Sweden and Subregions, *Ambio.* Vol 28 No. 7, pp. 604–612.

Wackernagel, Mathis, William Rees (1996): Our Ecological Footprint: Reducing Human Impact on the Earth. New Society Publishers, Gabriola Island, BC (available via Central Books, London, or directly from the publishers: Fax ++1-250 2477471, E-Mail: *nsp@island.net,* Price: USD 14.95;). Alternatively, visit the Web page: http://www.edg.net.mx/~mathiswa or http://www.rprogress.org, which provide more information and a list of scientific publications.

Wada, Yoshihiko (1993): The Appropriated Carrying Capacity of Tomato Production: The Ecological Footprint of Hydroponic Green-house versus Mechanized Open Field Operations. M.A. Thesis. School of Community and Regional Planning, University of British Columbia, Vancouver.

WBCSD (1996): Eco-Efficiency Leadership, Geneva: World Business Council for Sustainable Development. Geneva: World Business Council for Sustainable Development (WBCSD).

WEF (1997): Global Competitiveness Report 1997, Geneva: World Economic Forum, http://www.weforum.org/publications/gcr, accessed on 9.4.98.

WEF (1998): Africa Competitiveness Report 1998, Geneva: World Economic Forum, http://www.weforum.org/publications/acr, accessed on 9.4.98.

Authors

Dr. Andreas Sturm
Partner of Ellipson Ltd., a leading environmental consulting group in Basel, Switzerland. In that capacity, he has worked with small and medium sized companies, large global players, the United Nations (UNCTAD, UN-ISAR: Standardised, Environmental Performance Indicators), the OECD (Greener Public Purchasing), and government authorities (implementation of energy taxes and refund systems). Dr. Sturm has lectured at the University of Basel, is a regular guest lecturer at the Asian Institute of Technology (AIT)/ School of Management (SOM) in Thailand and at the Vienna University of Economics and Business Administration in Austria on the subject of "Corporate Environmental Management." He holds a Masters degree in business administration (lic. oec. HSG) and a Ph. D. in public policy (Dr. rer. pol.).

Dr. Mathis Wackernagel
Director of the sustainability program at Redefining Progress, a San Francisco-based nonprofit, nonpartisan public policy institute. He also directs the Centre for Sustainability Studies at An·huac University of Xalapa, Mexico. He has worked on sustainability issues for organisations in France, Canada, Costa Rica, Mexico, Switzerland, and the United States and has lectured for community groups, NGOs, and at more than 70 universities in 17 countries. Dr. Wackernagel holds a Ph. D. in community and regional planning, and is one of the two originators of the "ecological footprint" concept, now a widely used measure of sustainability.

Kaspar Müller
Founder and partner of Ellipson AG. His expertise is financial analysis, investment policy, value-oriented management, and sustainable strategies. He serves on the board of Ethos, a Swiss pension fund for sustainable development, and on the board of SVFV (Swiss Association of Financial Analysis and Investment Management), he co-chairs the Commission on Financial Accounting of EFFAS (European Federation of Financial Analysts' Societies)

and is a member of FER (Committee on Accounting; Swiss-GAAP). From 1980 to 1989, he was financial analyst, member of the strategic planning committee and the head of corporate finance at a Swiss private bank. From 1987 to 1994 he was president of the Shareholder Information Committee. He has consulted with various companies and organisations (UNCTAD, UN-ISAR: Standardised, Environmental Performance Indicators, the OECD Greener Public Purchasing). Mr. Müller holds a Masters degree in economics (lic. rer. pol.) from the University of Basel (Switzerland).

Contact Addresses

Dr. Andreas Sturm
Ellipson Ltd.
Leonhardsgraben 52
CH-4051 Basel
Switzerland
Website: http://www.ellipson.com
E-mail: *sturm@ellipson.com*
Fax: (+41-61) 261 93 13
Telephone: (0+41-61) 263 93 92

Dr. Mathis Wackernagel
Indicators Program at Redefining Progress
and
Centro de Estudios para la Sustentabilidad at the Universidad
Anáhuac de Xalapa
Postal address:
Redefining Progress
One Kearny Street, 4th Floor
San Francisco, CA 94108 U.S.A.
Website: http://www.rprogress.org
Website: http://www.edg.net.mx/~mathiswa
E-mail: *wackernagel@rprogress.org*
Fax: (+1-415) 781 11 98
Telephone: (+1-415) 781 11 91 ext. 317

Kaspar Müller
Ellipson Ltd.
Leonhardsgraben 52
CH-4051 Basel
Switzerland
Website: http://www.ellipson.com
E-mail: *mueller@ellipson.com*
Fax: (+41-61) 261 93 13
Telephone: (0+41-61) 263 93 91

Notes

1 See interview with her in Motavalli (1999).
2 This contradiction is prominently discussed in the debate between
   environmental scientist Norman Myers and the late economist Julian L. Simon (1994).
3 The corresponding electronic document with tables in Excel 4.0
   format can be found on the server of the International Council for
   Local Environmental Initiatives (ICLEI). Go to the homepage
   http://www.iclei.org, where you will find a "footprint" reference or
   go directly to: http://www.iclei.org/iclei/efcalcs.htm.
4 In the following countries, we have had direct contact with acade-
   mics using the footprint concept in their teaching or their research
   projects: Argentina, Australia, Austria, Canada, Chile, China, Colombia, Costa Rica, Denmark, Ecuador, England, Finland, Germany,
   Guernsey, Hong Kong, Ireland, Italy, Japan, Lithuania, Mexico, the
   Netherlands, New Zealand, Philippines, Portugal, Scotland, Singapore, Spain, Sweden, Switzerland, Taiwan, Turkey, Uruguay, and the
   U.S.A. Many academic papers and theses analysing the footprint
   concept or applying it to the researchers' own regions have been
   published. Now, Prof. Robert Costanza is hosting a special forum
   on footprints in *Ecological Economics*. Also, many high school curricula are incorporating footprints. For example, the footprint is
   now a part of the official school curriculum in the province of On-
   tario, Canada.
5 Outside the U.S.A., these municipal green plan initiatives are kno-
   wn under the name of "Local Agenda 21". These local agendas represent the municipal responses to the "Agenda 21" brought forward at the Earth Summit of Rio de Janeiro in 1992.
6 Many Agenda 21 initiatives have used ecological footprints in their
   communications of the sustainability challenges. For example, the
   municipality of the Hague in the Netherlands has developed a crea-
   tive brochure on footprints. Governments have also begun to refer
   to the footprint in their documents. For instance, this year the Ja-
   panese government released a white-paper that talks about footprints. Or the Dutch Environmental Minister Jan Pronk (who has
   mentioned footprints in many of his speeches) has asked his advi-

sory committee to identify the policy implications of footprints for Holland. It also has stimulated the discussion with other initiatives to promote sustainability such as the Natural Step (Holmberg et al. 1999).

7 Examples include the study presented in this book, van Vuuren et al. (1999) or Wackernagel et al. (1997, 1999a, 1999b).

8 Examples include Wackernagel (1998) or Davidson and Robb (1994).

9 Examples are Wackernagel and Richardson 1998, Deumling et al. (1999) or Best Foot Forward from Oxford. The latter has developed various footprint-based assessment software packages, including *Eco-Cal* and *Eco-Cal for Schools*. For details visit: http://www.bestfootforward.com.

10 Examples are Wada (1993) and Kautsky et al. (1997). See also Best Foot Forward's example of footprinting Danish beverage systems.

11 Today about 3 percent of the bio-productive area of our planet is protected as national parks. Conservation biologists believe, however, that, independent of questions of the relative justice of claims between various species of plant and animals and solely for the utilitarian aim of the protection of species, a substantially larger area should be protected. After examining numerous studies, the conservation ecologist and scientific director of the Wildland Project, Reed Noss, and Allen Cooperrider reach the conclusion that most regions should reserve between 25 and 75 percent of their area for eco-reserves and buffer zones – assuming that the protected area is ideally situated and linked by ecological corridors. For further discussions, consult Noss and Cooperrider 1994.

12 The calculations of the ecological footprint and the ecological capacity refer to the year 1993. At the point when this study was started, 1993 was the last year for which all required data was available for all countries.

13 The gross domestic product (GDP) figures are purchasing-power-adjusted in U.S. dollars (USD) at the values of 1993.

14 Conventional wisdom suggests that there is a decreasing marginal benefit for implementing eco-efficiency, meaning the more ecologically efficiently a company performs, the more expensive any further improvements may become. Paul Hawken, Amory Lovins, and Hunter Lovins, however, maintain that industrialised countries are

still far from reaching these limits since quite spectacular resource efficiency improvements have not yet been exploited (Hawken, Lovins, and Lovins 1999).

15 The competitiveness of nations is influenced by a wide range of factors, such as the level of education and income, infrastructure, political stability, etc. These factors are regularly summarised by the "World Economic Forum" in Geneva to give an index of competitiveness (WEF 1997). This index is used here as a measurement of competitiveness: The methodology is based on a Competitiveness Index that summarises the structural characteristics of an economy that determines prospects for medium-term growth. These include open markets, lean government spending, low tax rates, flexible labour markets, a stable political system, and an effective judiciary (WEF 1998).

16 In the case of France, a large question mark has to be added due to the high proportion of nuclear energy. This energy policy could prove to be a heavy ecological and economic encumbrance. If this should be the case, competitiveness would suffer severely.

17

Definitions	Classification
• Eco-efficient: footprint per unit gross domestic product (purchasing power adjusted at 1993 prices) [ha/USD] • Capacity reserves: footprint per capita minus capacity per capita [ha] • Relative footprint: footprint per capita [ha] • Wealth: gross domestic product per capita (purchasing power adjusted at 1993 prices) [USD] • Competitiveness: World Economic Forum Index 1997	• Eco-Efficiency Leader: eco-efficiency above average Eco-Efficiency Laggards: eco-efficiency below average • Creditor: footprint smaller than capacity Debtor: footprint larger than capacity • Little feet: footprint per capita below average Big feet: footprint per capita above average • GDP per capita: 80–100%: very high GDP per capita: 60–70%: high GDP per capita: 40–60%: medium GDP per capita: 20–40%: low GDP per capita: 0–20%: very low (expressed in % of the GDP range) • Competitive: WEF-Index larger than 0 Not competitive: WEF-Index smaller 0 (see note 12 on calculations)

18 Much work exists on how market mechanisms could be used for enhancing countries' environmental performance (see for example Sterner 1999). Redefining Progress is running a number of projects

on possible mechanisms to advance more sustainable incentive systems. This includes initiatives on environmental tax reform (see http://www.rprogress.org/pubs/greengold/greengold_execsum.html) and auctioning atmospheric user rights (see http://www. rprogress. org/progsum/rip/dga/dga_main.html). An intriguing approach is also Peter Barnes's proposal to develop a sky trust (Barnes 1999 or visit http://www.skytrust.cfed.org).

19 The higher the price of the certificate, the lower the average footprint will get. Eventually, the overall footprint has to shrink to the size of the biosphere or to take 1993 population numbers, from the average of 2.65 hectares per person to no higher than 2 hectares per person (and lower if the world population continues to grow). To achieve this with minimum disruption, the certificate prices could be increased slowly over time.

20 See Ehrlich et al. 1999 for an additional discussion on the limitations of innovation.

21 In order to avoid undesired effects (misallocations), these instruments should be designed so that the total national budget does not have more money available than it would have without these instruments (state quota neutrality) and that the revenue is reimbursed to the population and the companies. Should international cooperation not be brought about, the introduction of these instruments may be designed neutrally in terms of foreign trade. However, the full potential use would not then be exploited.